Writes of Passage:

WRITING THROUGH THE SEASONS OF YOUR LIFE

by Marjorie St. Clair

ISBN: 9798698254300

Earth Muse Press
2000 Aina Mahi'ai St.
Lahaina, Maui, 96761

ACKNOWLEDGMENTS

In appreciation to all those who have taken my *Writes of Passage* classes over the years, inspiring me with their amazing stories and heartfelt writing; to my family and friends who have inspired and supported me through my own rites of passage, especially my daughter Suzanne; to my ancestors who walked and roamed the Celtic Isles for centuries before coming to America in the early 1700s and who imbued me with an abiding love of music and storytelling; to my Native American mentor & teacher Beautiful Painted Arrow/Joseph Rael; to author-teacher of the Hopi Indians, Robert Boissiere and the Kaywena family of Hopi's Second Mesa and to Keeper of the Fire Clan Tablets, the Hopi elder Martin or Titus of Hotevilla; to Pete & Isabel Concho of the Taos Pueblo; and to Mayan scholar, author & friend Jose Arguelles. I am grateful for the wisdom, time, & patience they all imparted to me over the many years of friendship & how they helped me to remember through ritual, prayer, ceremony & vision quest, my own ancient pagan roots in Mother Earth.

To my beloved Buddhist teacher, the Reverend Zen Master Gilbert of San Francisco whom I first met & interviewed as a guest on a television talk show I hosted in Huntsville, AL. He taught me by example what it means to walk humbly and with great kindness.

To my artistic book designer and technology whizz, Denise Weaver Ross, whose constant help has been invaluable. To all the talentend women writers who allowed me to include examples of their writing in this book: Jo Bryant, Shirley Chavez, Ana Leite Powell, Sandy King, Rebecca Leeman, Dairne McLoughlin, Carey McDonald, and Elizabeth Prosapio.

Finally, to the Great Sisterhood of Wild Women & Wise Women who have tendered my life with their deep river of compassion and without whose love this long earth journey would not have sparkled with the magic and miracles they so generously sprinkled about at every twist and turn, meeting me where and when I most needed it.

It is my hope that everyone who is drawn to this book will find it illuminating & helpful as they experience through its written exercises, visualizations and art, fresh eyes to appreciate the amazing lives they've led.

TABLE OF CONTENTS

Writes of Passage:

WRITING THROUGH THE SEASONS OF YOUR LIFE

by Marjorie St. Clair

INTRODUCTION

Those masterful images because complete
Grew in pure mind, but out of what began?
A mound of refuse or the sweepings of a street,
Old kettles, old bottles, and a broken can,
Old iron, old bones, old rags, that raving slut
Who keeps the till. Now that my ladder's gone,
I must lie down where all the ladders start,
In the foul rag-and-bones shop of the heart.
...W.B. Yeats

Years before I began teaching creative writing, I facilitated and led women's personal rites of passage through wilderness vision quests. During rites of passage as practiced by traditional cultures, specific rituals such as the vision quest are used to assist individuals in becoming aware of their life's purpose by returning to nature and asking for a vision. I was inspired to lead rites of passage using vision quests and other wilderness experiences as a way to give back to others what have been life-changing experiences of my own in nature and during vision quests. One of the important lessons I learned during my years as a participant and later as a guide was nature's mysterious power to assist and guide an individual into a more receptive and balanced state of mine. Over the years I came to understand that nature is a teacher in her own right and that once we learn to listen, deeply listen, to her and follow her instructions, even when they seem "wrong" or crazy, they lead us to experiences we may never have dreamed possible. I also experienced in my personal life how the power of rituals used in rites of passage were able to ease the stress from the accelerated pace of life and often led to a deeper understanding and healing of our inner psyches, especially during periods of radical personal and global transition and change.

When I first started teaching creative writing, I asked students to keep a journal, either as a source of creative ideas for use in their storytelling or as a means to get their creative juices flowing. Journal writing, I said, could also be used as a place to record their personal lives. Whenever students shared their journal writing, I was continually amazed at the deeply felt emotions they expressed and of the catharsis that followed after the expunging of negative experiences detailed through their journal writing. From sexual abuse, alcoholism and drug addiction, living on the streets, to religious traumas, participants were experiencing transformative insights into the painful events in their lives, either for the first time or at a level they hadn't accessed before. I knew from my own journal keeping over the years that writing in a journal is a cathartic experience that can lead to personal insights, understanding and forgiveness, and sometimes to love and compassion. To share those written experiences in a group setting, I observed, only heightened those experiences.

The evolution of *Writes of Passage: Writing Through the Seasons of Your Life* began when I started to wonder if peoples' life experiences during the cycles of personal development could be assisted and integrated more easily by combining the two healing processes of rites of passage journey experiences with journal writing. I realized that not everyone could physically go on a vision quest and that perhaps, by combining these two forms of healing and self-expression, it would give people a means to explore, understand and accept their life's experiences, both good and bad, while also giving them a written record, much like creating a visual road map of their lives. Combining these two healing modalities I thought could also provide insightful ways for moving forward in one's life with confidence and clarity, especially in the last cycle of life.

The first *Writes of Passage: Writing Through the Seasons of Your Life* workbook, one of many that evolved as time went on, grew out of these initial ideas and during actual classes in which participants offered their ideas through their writing and creativity.

In working with and evolving the *Writes of Passage* stories and writing exercises, I was able to see how writing assists people to get in touch with and reclaim buried and unhealed parts of themselves abandoned during painful or traumatic experiences in their life, especially in the early years, a time when personal identities are being shaped. What I observed from most participants' writing was a profound recognition and healing of past events, followed by an experience of joy as a result of writing out, past and through their traumas.

I have learned that people have a burning desire to write the story of their lives because they realize that no matter how ordinary they may think their lives have seemed, their story is unique to them and deserves to be told. I have also learned that people want to tell their stories to experience the letting go and catharsis that comes by sharing those dark nights of the soul with their fellow human beings whom they soon realize are also on the same journey.

People are caring, responsible and sincerely want to live lives of purpose and meaning. Astonishingly, all these elements were revealed through peoples' writing in the *Writes of Passage* workbook, as week after week they would make a journey together while experiencing a growing trust and respect for one another as they courageously exhumed through their writing the most potent memories and feelings about themselves and the "seasons of their own lives!"

The guided writing journal experience, I discovered, was the perfect way to give people the unique opportunity to write, and then reflect on what they'd written. This process opens people up to new possibilities for responding to others in more positive ways and to the events in their life with a truer sense of an authentic self and of their life's purpose.

It has always been important to me that participants in any writing class or retreat I offer be able to engage in a variety of other forms of creativity. With this in mind, throughout the six distinct phases of the writes, or rites, of passage journey, there are numerous opportunities to make art for pleasure and fun as an additional way for getting in touch with the imagination and learning to give voice to a greater creative potential that exists in everyone and further deepens our lives and enlarges our perspectives as to what's possible.

Writing in the *Writes of Passages* workbook and following the exercises in each of the six phases is a way to increase personal awareness of old patterns of behavior in making decisions, while offering insights into how we respond to others and how we can shape our ideas and dreams for our future.

As I developed and tweaked the writing exercises for the six phases, a gradual organic unfolding began to occur, with each exercise evolving from and building on or adding to the ones preceding it.

Here then is a brief summary of the six phases of the *Writes of Passage: Writing Through the Seasons of Your Life* workbook:

Phase One on the writes of passage journey is called *Youth, Identity and Finding Your Way*. Here we look at the stages of development all humans are thought to experience as they grow into mature adults. Because myths are a direct conduit for imparting a culture's traditions and provide specific guidance for journeying through various life stages of development, they are an important aspect of how we find our way. Myths of the hero's journey, for example, are studied for gaining a better understanding of the importance of symbols and archetypes and because they offer a template for our own personal story or myth. Through reflection on one particular ancient myth called *The Seal Maiden*, we are reminded of the reality of soul-loss and what the consequences of such a loss can be. By reflective writing about the characters and events in the story, we gain a personal perspective of soul-loss by examining our own lives and events in our past. Our artistic side is also given an opportunity to express itself when we create a Life Map showing all the important events in our life, followed by the creation of a poem using a template called "Where I'm From."

Phase Two of our journey is called *Gathering Wisdom and Honoring Your Ancestors*. What are the wisdom traditions from which we draw our knowledge and values about who we are and what is important to us? In answering these and other questions, we look at spiritual and philosophical thoughts, ideas, and stories worldwide to inspire and teach us. We become especially mindful of the gifts our ancestors have bestowed upon us as we re-discover our inheritance by excavating personal family histories. We write about our ancestral roots as a way to reconnect to who we are and where we came from, and to trace the stories and traditions that influenced our families. By writing about a special ancestor and creating an altar or special place of honor for them in our home, we invoke their presence in our daily lives, giving us a source of strength and continuity to our past.

Phase Three is called *Letting Go—Writing Through to Completions in Your Life*. This is the place known in traditional rites of passage journeys as the *severance* phase. It is the time for attending to attitudes and habits that hold us back from walking fully into our wholeness. As our conscious attention turns to the process of letting go, we become aware of ourselves as persons who are living in the here and now and that the letting go process requires courageous truth telling, forgiveness and compassion towards others as well as ourselves. Numerous writing exercises and reflection on readings assist us in taking the steps necessary to complete any unfinished business in our lives and to let go of people or circumstances which no longer serve us.

Phase Four, *Finding the Soul of Your Work—Writing Past Fear to Your Passion*, provides the opportunity to take a good look at re-discovering our personal calling in life. It is closely tied to the former cycle of letting go. Through our writing, we become more acutely aware of what inner work we must do to find our soul's purpose. We are inspired by the thoughts of psychologist James Hillman and his "acorn theory" for living an authentic life. As we delve into the question of "what do I really want?"

we make a Treasure Map, write a "found poem," and finally, reflect on and write about three possible future paths we might choose that will nurture us at a soul level.

Putting Your Wisdom to Work: Making an Act of Power is **Phase Five** and, in rites of passage traditions, is a cycle of *threshold* and *transformation*. Through meditation, visualization, written exercises and art making, we imagine what our act of power might look like and how we can put it out into the world.

Becoming an Elder: Loving Yourself and Serving Others, **Phase Six**, asks us to consider our own aging and death. In this phase, we look to the wisdom writings from ancient cultures that do not fear death but welcome it as simply another rite of passage from one cycle of existence to another. Through writing exercises, reflective reading and visualization, we investigate and revisit our dreams of the past and what things we still want to pursue; how we can mentor and influence others as we age; and how we would like to be remembered.

Author with her former students at Salam Academy

PHASE ONE
Youth, Identity & Finding Your Way

*If you follow your bliss, you put yourself on a kind of track, which has been there all the while
waiting for you, and the life that you ought to be living is the one you are living.*
... Joseph Campbell

*It takes a universe to make a child, both in outer form
and inner spirit. It takes a universe to educate a child, a universe to fulfill a child.*
... Thomas Berry

Personal Development During Stages of Our Life

Personal development in the West has been identified as occurring in specific stages: early childhood, adolescence, adult and elder, with certain events marking each stage. Our personal identities are the amalgam of our experiences on all levels of the psyche as we traverse through these stages, which include the physical, emotional, mental and spiritual aspects of our being. Many traditional cultures have in place a system for navigating these passages of personal growth known as rites of passage. We in the West, however, have lost knowledge of these special rites and often do very little to mark or celebrate the important transitions in our lives beyond those of birth, graduation, marriage, new baby or death.

Through the writing you will do in the *Writes of Passage: Writing Through the Seasons of Your Life* workbook, you will make note of your own major rites of passages by looking to your past and remembering those significant experiences and events that have made you who you are today while learning to view them as significant markers along your life's journey, which also reflects your present and extends into your future.

Initiations for the Young

In ancient times and in today's more traditional cultures, transitions from childhood to becoming an adult and then an elder were assisted and acknowledged by the community through rites of passage. Participation in a rite of passage included an awareness of the work that had to be done to pass from one cycle to the next, and occurred in the following stages: *preparation, severance and purification, threshold and transformation,* and *finally return and reincorporation.* Often called an initiation, most rites of passage rituals were carried out by elders of the tribe or community as a way to assist the young in making the difficult passage from youth into adulthood, often requiring that the youth endure certain hardships of the body, such as hunger or thirst from prolonged fasting, and by spending time alone in wilderness. As a result of these experiences, the initiate would often transcend into a heightened sense of awareness, resulting in clear dreaming or visions. These dreams, which were thought to be a source of revelation given to the person to help them discover their soul's purpose, were told to the elders who helped in interpreting them.

Similarly, in ancient Greece, we know that women initiates were led into caves where they remained alone for several days as they sought to know themselves in deeper ways. They were instructed to dream, while alternatively bathing in nearby waters to renew themselves by washing away any inhibiting emotions or attitudes of childhood in preparation for becoming an adult, usually denoting becoming a mother who would give birth to a child or children or become a priestess in service to the Goddess.

A Hopi Girl's Initiation: Grinding Corn

Wikimedia Commons: Public Domain

Initiations for the young are still important rites of passage for many Native Americans. During a trip to the Hopi Indian Reservation in Arizona some years ago, I had taken a group of women to visit Hopi friends living in the village of Shipalovi on Second Mesa. A young Hopi girl was going through her initiation into becoming an adult, and we were graciously, and surprisingly, invited by my Hopi hostess who was the young girl's aunt, to observe part of the ritual. We were led into one of the small adobe homes that surround the village plaza where the young girl was undergoing her initiation. Seated in the corner of a room beside a large stack of corn, the young girl had been grinding corn by hand for several days and nights. My Hopi friend told us that during her initiation the young girl had to remain in silence and she was only allowed a few hours of sleep. An older woman, usually a relative such as an aunt or cousin, was always in attendance while the initiate pursued her task of grinding corn. While we were there, the aunt of the young girl was present with her, standing over her ironing board and ironing clothes, all the while chanting softly under her breath.

"The corn ground by the young girl will be used in special ceremonies to bless dancers in the kiva," my friend told us. "We'll also use the corn she has ground to make our sacred piki bread that we'll serve to the entire village as part of the feast in her honor that will follow her initiation."

"Once the grinding of the massive quantities of corn is complete," she told us, "the girl will be bathed by her elders and dressed in ceremonial clothes made especially for her. Then we'll wash her hair with yucca soap made from the desert yucca plant and tie it up in the traditional way of Hopi women, with large spirals on either side of her head. Once she's ready, she'll be presented to the village."

We were all deeply moved by the beauty of the initiation ceremony for the young girl and the care and attention given to her by the entire community during her rite of passage.

Does Nature Play A Role In Human Development?

In his book *Nature and the Human Soul*, author Bill Plotkin presents a model of human development that includes the soul. It is a nature-based model that he calls a *Soulcentric Developmental Wheel*. It contains eight life stages that are arranged around a nature-based circle, in direct opposition to the Western linear timeline of human development. The stages of life in Plotkin's developmental model are independent of chronological age, biological changes, cognitive ability or social role. Movement from one stage to the next happens as

Wikimedia Commons: Public Domain

an individual progresses with the specific psychological and spiritual tasks encountered at each stage. In Plotkin's model, the developmental task that characterizes each stage is nature oriented but also includes the cultural aspect of the Western developmental model, requiring a balance between both nature and culture.

Plotkin believes that our lack of acknowledgement of our souls and alienation from nature are greater impediments to our maturation than the loss of meaningful rites of passage. He says that we live in a largely adolescent society because of centuries of cultural as well as environmental degradation that has left most humans never reaching true adulthood. According to Plotkin, this adolescent world of imbalance and immaturity is reflected in our materialistic, greedy, competitive, violent, racist, sexist and self-destructive contemporary societies. Plotkin's model is an attempt to present another way to come to maturity in which all aspects of our being are acknowledged, including our soul and the sacredness of the world we live in. He believes that it's not too late to change and in his book presents ways that people can reclaim what he calls "our full membership in this flowering planet and animated universe and become more fully human, both as individuals and as societies. We can grow unimpeded into adulthood and eventually, elderhood and create twenty-first century life-sustaining societies."[1]

---

1 Bill Plotkin, *Nature and the Human Soul*, pg. 6

Do Our Dreams Guide Us?

Teacher and author Normandi Ellis says in her beautifully written memoir *Dreaming Isis* that it is not the soul's way to adhere to chronology. "Our lives are formed and reformed out of memory," she tells us. "The stories appear when the time of their reckoning appears. I perceive dreams as texts of equal importance to the papyri of the ancient Egyptians themselves. All of it—the life, the dreams, the language, the events---are open to interpretation." It is important to keep in mind that many thinkers, like Ellis and Plotkin, do not see life as proceeding and developing in a straight line.

Nature-Deficit Disorder?

Author and educator Richard Louv has written almost a dozen books, his landmark work being *Last Child in the Woods: Saving Our Children from Nature-Deficit Disorder* in which he combines extensive research showing the correlation of exposure to nature as being essential for a child's healthy physical and emotional development. His evidence linking the lack of nature in a child's life to the rise in obesity, attention deficit disorders and depression generated an international back to nature campaign; giving rise to the motto, "leave no child inside."

At the beginning of Louv's book he quotes a fourth-grader from San Diego, "I like to play indoors better 'cause that's where all the electrical outlets are." Later, in a chapter called "The Best of Intentions: Why Johnnie and Jeannie Don't Play Outside Anymore," he tells us about the fear that many children have towards nature, something he observed again and again as he traveled across America doing his research. Louv also noted parent's fear of crime, abduction or stranger-dangers; fears that even extended to nature itself, preventing them from allowing their children the freedom they themselves enjoyed when they were young and growing up. The time that both adults and children now spend on electronic devices, he says, has not only reduced any time that in the past may have been spent outdoors enjoying the many wonders of nature, but has further diminished the possibility of quality, unstructured or free time in nature.

Louv believes that the coming decades will be a pivotal time in the direction our Western world takes in healing the broken bond between children and nature. While he believes that this will be an enormously challenging task, he doesn't think it's impossible and points to efforts being made across this country and throughout the world directed towards protecting the natural world because people understand that it is key to our health and well being, both physical as well as spiritual.

Can Myths Help In Human Development?

Myths have been used as a means to entertain people ever since our ancient kin sat around fires and told of the deeds of the day and of their heroic ancestors. Ancient myths and folk tales were originally stories about real people who under pressure did courageous and heroic deeds that over time became sources of wisdom for their descendants, offering ways to map the development of their psyches. When looked at in this way, myths assume a place beyond being true or false, right or wrong; rather they offer ways of organizing experience for the well being of an individual or group. According to many psychologists, sociologists and spiritual teachers, the importance of myths in shaping who we are can't be overestimated.

In particular, the mythic tales of the hero's journey were intended to transform an adolescent into an adult. Although hero myths vary in detail, they follow a similar structure for human development. Mythologist and scholar Joseph Campbell's first book, *The Hero with a Thousand Faces*, focused on the hero's journey and how to read a myth not as "something that happened out there but as something that is going to happen to you and is happening to you, that's translating this material into spiritual food." Campbell was intent on helping us understand that "myths have to do with how you live your life" and that myths do matter! In 1987 a film about Campbell and his work called *The Hero's Journey* premiered at the Museum of Modern Art in New York, and was followed in 1988 by the television series on PBS, *The Power of Myth,* that features interviews of Joseph Campbell by Bill Moyers. Seemingly overnight, Campbell's message that "the first and most essential service of a mythology is this one: of opening the mind and heart to the utter wonder of all being" struck a chord with millions of people worldwide and the study of myths and mythology was back on the table.

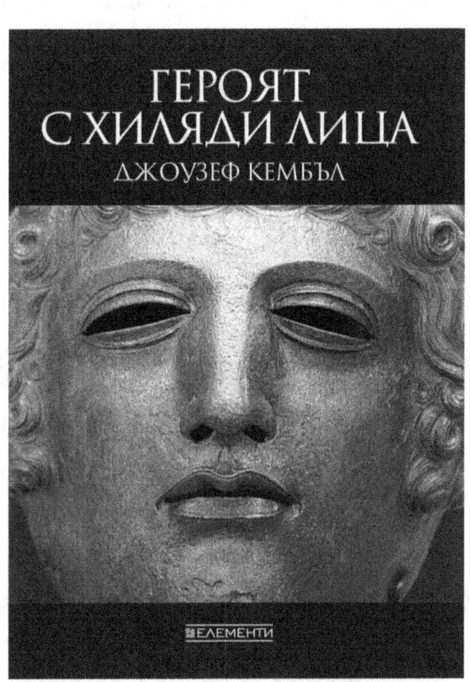

Cover image of the Bulgarian first edition of Joseph Campbell's book, "The Hero of a Thousand Faces "
CC BY-SA / creativecommons.org/licenses/by-sa/4.0

Psychologist Rollo May, for example, says in his book *The Cry for Myth* that "myths are narrative patterns that give significance to our existence, and give us ways to find meaning and significance."

Writing Your Own Hero/Heroine Story

Hollywood screenwriter and writing teacher Christopher Vogler developed a model for writing using what he calls a "mythic structure," based on his study of the hero's journey developed through the work and research of famous mythologist and author Joseph Campbell. In his book *The Writer's Journey: Mythic Structure for Writers*, Vogler combines the theory of archetypes as developed by Carl Jung with the components of the classic hero's myth as Campbell developed and applied them to the creation of modern stories. The hero's tale is always a journey, he writes, whether it is an outward physical journey or an inward journey of the mind, heart and soul. And, as in any good story, the hero or heroine grows and changes, moving from weakness to strength, from foolishness to wisdom and from hate to love.

Stages of the Hero's Journey

Vogler defines the stages of the hero's journey in this way: first we see the hero in his/her *ordinary world* where they live; then the hero receives a *call to an adventure* of some kind but often isn't ready or is afraid and refuses the call. This leads to the hero meeting a Mentor who will help her accept the call; the hero *crosses the first threshold* into another reality or world unknown to him; in this *non-ordinary world* the hero undergoes tests of danger, bravery, and wisdom while being assisted by allies and assaulted by enemies; the hero approaches the innermost cave where the *ultimate ordeal* that he must undergo awaits him; there, he wins the reward or treasure by his bravery and cunning; then, after he has experienced a *resurrection or rebirth*, he takes the road back to his former world and *returns with the elixir or treasure*, which he shares for the good of all the community.

Vogler tells us that when we try and heal with the wisdom of myth, we are kin to the shamans of old who asked the same questions presented by the myths: "Who am I? Where did I come from? What happens when I die? What does it mean? Where do I fit in? Where am I bound on my own hero's Journey?"

Mythologist Joseph Campbell spent years studying and documenting world myths, especially the hero myths that appear in classical Greece, Rome, the Middle East, and Asia that extend down to contemporary cultures of today. The hero's journey unfolds over a distinct period of time, lasting from months to years and leads the man or woman involved on an adventure that necessitates their entering the mysterious realm of the psyche or soul, to experience a psychological and spiritual death, followed by a rebirth and an eventual return to his or her "ordinary reality" with a new maturity and a life vision.

There is a difference in the hero's and heroine's journey, however: the male's journey follows a more linear unfolding, proceeding from one outward goal to the next, while the woman's journey bears a closer resemblance to a spiral that she travels, reaching into her center then expanding outward over and over again. Nevertheless, the obstacles, challenges, helpers, revelations, transformations, death and rebirths are common to both.

Creating Your Personal Myth

In seeking to understand our own personal cycles of soul, we often find that we behave and define ourselves according to a self-defeating myth that we may not consciously realize is failing us. Personal mythmaking is the primary, though often unperceived, psychological mechanism by which human beings navigate their way through life. For several years I created and taught a class called *Creating Your Personal Narrative* because I had long been observing the power of a positive personal myth to guide and shape our lives in self-affirming ways. A personal myth functions for the individual as cultural myths do for a community, and while you might think you don't have a personal myth, there is much evidence to the contrary. Think of the stories you're always telling friends or new people you meet, stories about your past and the people whom you've interacted with.

Wikimedia: Commons

Psychologists such as Erik Erikson believe that our self-identities are formed as we interpret experiences from the past in terms of the meaning they hold in our current lives. Whether we are conscious of it or not, we are continually creating an inner story to explain events from our past in an effort to better understand the present and prepare for the future. All of these individual events are registered in our psyches and are represented by certain archetypes and symbols that impact us over time in ways that both shape and help us to construct a personal mythology.

Personal Mythology: Using Ritual, Dreams, and Imagination to Discover Your Inner Story is a book by psychologists David Feinstein and Stanley Krippner that offers useful exercises, guided visualizations and specific ideas and information on how to work with personal mythology. Feinstein and Krippner describe a personal myth as having at its core a central theme that all new experiences organize around. It's a template or skeleton that imagery, beliefs, intense feelings and motivations attach themselves to. This personal myth is distinctive, guides our behavior, and helps us to evolve in the world. However, before we can work with that myth, the authors tell us, we must become aware of what that myth is. Once we become aware of our prevailing personal myth, and identify any outmoded or unproductive personal myths that may be operating outside our conscious awareness, we can begin to revise them.

During *Creating Your Personal Narrative* classes, members quickly saw how important, and sometimes difficult, it was to recognize their current guiding myth and to identify any harmful or destructive patterns; something they had to do before they could perceive a new, revised personal myth. Once they had observed and identified through their writing any harmful patterns they saw repeating themselves, they worked to develop a new personal myth to replace the self-defeating myth that was perpetuating the destructive patterns.

WRITING EXERCISE: Writing Your Life Story as a Three Part Myth

PART ONE: Writing Your Guiding Myth

Weaving your memories into a meaningful sequence of stories or personal narrative about your past can deepen your relationship with your own mythology. In order to recognize an area of your mythology that is failing you, begin by sensing that your current myth is not the only way to organize your life; that there is a larger story to be told.

Think of a time when you were young and recall an event in which you experienced deep feelings or emotions as a result of a conflict or trauma. Write about this event, including the setting, who was there with you, being as specific as possible. Then, using the specifics of the events that we are calling self-defeating, write a short myth of your early self, beginning with "Once upon a time..." It can be as long as a page or as short as two or three paragraphs. Seeing yourself as the hero or heroine in your own personal narrative allows you to look more closely into your nature and to appreciate more fully the wonder of the human drama as it manifests in your personal story. In this first exercise, you will focus on identifying aspects of a self-defeating myth present in your life that may still be functioning as your guiding myth. Write your Guiding Myth in the space below:

____

____

____

____

____

____

____

____

____

____

Here is an example of *Part One, Your Guiding Myth* written by a participant named Sandy from the class *Creating Your Own Personal Narrative*:

Your Guiding Myth

Once upon a time there lived a little girl, let's call her "Alice in Wonderland." She just loved being in nature, collecting insects, fascinated with anything that crawled. She could spend hours in the woods, running after butterflies, or if visiting the ocean, swimming and collecting shells. She adored her grandmother, and loved to spend time with her.

All would have been perfect except for the difficult relationship Alice had with her mother. It's as if they were from different planets. Her mother was very concerned with what others might think, and so her daughter Alice had to be this perfectly groomed, quiet, smiling and obedient child. The reality was very different, however, because Alice often would get dirty. She even had temper tantrums at a very young age. As soon as she was able to speak, she asked her mother deep questions about the universe and life, questions that most adults would marvel at. But these only made her mother uncomfortable and so she'd avoid answering them, instead she would tell Alive, "Go outside and play with the other kids. And don't be so serious. You need to lighten up and laugh more Alice."

The effect of these responses caused Alice to feel confused and ashamed that she was somehow different, flawed. She began to shut down, eventually shutting her mother out of her life. When told to kiss her parents goodnight, Alice would often refuse. Over time she became a quiet, secretive person, afraid to expose her real interests for fear of being ridiculed. This anger turned inward, festered and would later emerge in various unpleasant ways, including outbursts of anger, various skin conditions, including malignant cancerous growths and moodiness.

One day her grandmother said to her, "Alice, I'm so disappointed in you. You've changed and aren't the sweet child you used to be."

PART TWO: Writing Your Counter Myth

In the second writing exercise for your 3-part life myth, you will write
a counter-myth to the one you wrote in Part One. When an area of your
personal mythology becomes outdated for your circumstances or level of
psychological development, your psyche will generate alternative mythic
stories, or counter myths. Because counter myths are formed largely
in reaction to shortcomings of your prevailing myth, they contain their
own distortions, resulting in conflict between the two.

In this exercise, you will write another myth, this time showing how your
life has gone as a result of lashing out against the conflict and trauma that
happened in Part One. Look at the example below to see how Sandy wrote her counter-myth. When
writing your own counter myth, ask yourself these questions: How did I respond to the self-defeating
myth generated in my early childhood? What specific behaviors and attitudes did I take on as a result
of fighting against and rebutting the story in Part One? Write your Counter Myth in the space below:

____

____

____

____

____

____

____

____

____

____

____

____

____

Here is Sandy's example of *Part Two, A Counter Myth*:

Your Counter Myth

One day Alice climbed the tree outside her house, did a few flips through the air, landing on the garage, then off onto a flying star and to another planet! There she immediately felt at home. People were pursuing their own interests and were enthusiastic to share their passions. Everyone's eyes were sparkling and alive. It seemed they were attuned to life and to the creative energy of the universe. It was very exciting and energizing for Alice.

No one had to worry about paying bills or working at a job they hated. It was pretty idyllic. The neighborhoods were beautifully green, the beaches clean and the ocean inviting. What a paradise!

When it was time to leave, Alice once again boarded her flying star and off, off and away back to her earthly home. She was revitalized and ready to pursue a new life, influenced by this touch of possibility.

PART THREE: Writing Your New Personal Myth

Because there are shortcomings and strengths in both your old myth and your counter myth, you will write another story that incorporates the most vital aspects of both. First, review what you wrote in part one and part two. Now, using them as references, write a new, more accurate and empowering personal myth that takes the best from part one and part two. Be spontaneous and remember that this is a myth and you are the hero/heroine! Write you New Personal Myth below:

Here is Sandy's *Part Three* of her *New Personal Myth:*

New Personal Myth

Alice is living in community with like-minded people of all ages. It is an eco-village that has a light footprint on the earth. People help with chores and they meet for group meals a few times a week and yet they all have their own privacy when needed. This has changed Alice's life. She is feeling very safe and grounded. She is able to be herself. It's in a gorgeous area with four seasons, plenty of hiking close by, classes in yoga, Qi gong, various spiritual teachers passing through town stop by on a regular basis.

Alice has friends, as well as a marvelous therapist when she needs to talk about issues, which are mostly about her relationship with her mother. She is working on forgiving her mother and with all the support in her life, it's much easier to regain composure and let go of the anger. Alice attended a special LIGHT cleansing that got rid of a lot of her old patterns and addictions. Her cells are cleansed and with a positive outlook, healthy diet of food and thoughts, all things are possible She is even doing regular meditation again and finding comfort in the silence.

She is taking singing lessons and is overcoming her fear of expressing herself. She dreams more often and loves it when she awakes to realize she's had an experience while dreaming. It adds another dimension to her life. She enjoys reading and writing, and loves to have a project to work on. She is very satisfied with her life these days. And, in being happier, she is able to share her joy with others. What she has created is a life full of optimism but firmly grounded in community and spirituality.

The Seal Maiden: A Heroine's Journey Myth

One popular myth of a heroine's journey that is told worldwide is called *The Seal Maiden*. It tells the story of a young seal woman who has her sealskin stolen by a lonely fisherman who promises to return it to her in seven years if she will marry him. She agrees and follows him home to his village. The adventures that unfold as a result of the loss of her sealskin and her efforts to get it back provide many insights into what it means to lose part of your soul and the struggle to regain it. Just as the seal woman suffers from the loss of her sealskin in the story, we too can dry out, become deeply tired, go blind and loose our ability to walk and make our way in the world if we lose our soul. We will use writing as our tool of exploration into the themes and archetypes in this story to reclaim our lost or stolen sealskins and find our way back home to our soul place.

Although there are many versions and names for this story, I adapted this version from stories of the *selkie* people as told in Norway and the Scottish Isles, where large colonies of seals live offshore. Here, then, is the story of the seal maiden, or *selkie* as the seal folks are called.

The Seal Maiden

It came to pass one fine day that a Fisherman was down at the sea's edge when the tide was low and he happened to see a group of selkie-folk laying on a flat rock a short distance away. Some of the selkie-folk were sunning themselves on the rock while others were jumping and playing in the clear blue water. All were naked and had unblemished skin as white as snow. Their magical sealskins, which some say were enchanted, were strewn carelessly about on the sand and on nearby rocks.

The Fisherman crept closer to take a look at the selkies and as he did so, they spotted him. Quickly, they grabbed their sealskins and dove back into the safety of the sea. All but one beautiful seal maiden, that is. The Fisherman had managed to grab her sealskin in the rush and as she jumped into the sea without her sealskin, she fixed her gaze on him. With mournful eyes she seemed to beg him to give back her sealskin. Gazing back at her he realized in that moment that all but she had transformed themselves back into seals. With the sealskin tucked under his arm, he hastily headed back toward his home when he heard a sorrowful wailing and weeping coming from behind him. It was the seal maiden who had followed him and she began pleading with him to return her sealskin. He turned to look at the beautiful creature and watched as tears ran down her snow-white cheeks from her large, dark eyes.

Suddenly, he was filled with a passion he had never known. He decided to make the seal maiden a bargain, promising that if she married him and bore him children, he would return her seal skin in seven years and she would be free to return to her home in the sea. Of course, the seal maiden had little choice and agreed to the Fisherman's terms.

The Selkie woman bore the Fisherman two beautiful children, one boy and one girl. She was a good wife and seemed to be quite happy and content with her life with the Fisherman. But, things are not always as they seem and the Selkie woman longed to return to her home in the sea and her family there. She began to spend long hours gazing longingly out to sea and soon began to suffer from her years of time on the land. She began to go blind without the sea's healing moisture and she walked with a hobble as her legs and feet slowly began to swivel up. She would have to return to her rightful home in the sea very soon or she would die.

But she could not find where the Fisherman had hidden her sealskin, and although the seven years had passed, he refused to give it back to her. She looked high and she looked low but nowhere was her sealskin to be found. One day the Fisherman went out to fish with his son and forgot to take the key to the special box where he kept the sealskin hidden, locked and tucked away in the attic space above the bed. As the Selkie wife began to look up and down for her sealskin, her daughter asked, "What are you looking for mother?"

"Daughter. I'm looking for a special sealskin to make shoes for your pretty little feet," replied the Selkie mother, not wanting to alarm her daughter.

"Oh, I know where father keeps a very pretty sealskin, mother. I've watched many a time when you were away and father thought I was asleep. He takes a pretty sealskin out and stares at it for a while and then folds it and puts it back in a box he keeps in the attic over the bed. Today, he has left the key on the table," the daughter answered, reaching to pick up the key and handing it to her mother.

"Thank you daughter," the astonished Selkie mother said, clapping her hands with joy as she rushed to open the box.

As soon as the seal maiden took her sealskin from the box, she put it on and ran towards the sea, where she plunged into the waves with cries of joy. Once in the sea, she turned back into her selkie form and swam through the waves to a selkie man who was waiting for her. Before she swam away for good, however, she turned to her daughter waiting at the seashore and called out to her, "I will never forget you, my beautiful daughter, and I promise to return every year to visit with you and your brother. But I must return to the sea or I will die. Farewell." With that, the selkie woman swam away with the selkie man.

The Fisherman, returning in his small boat with his son from their day of fishing, happened to notice two seals in the distance. As the seals swam closer to his boat, one of them said, "Farewell Fisherman husband and my dear, darling boy. I must return to my home in the sea or perish. I will see you dear son once a year when I will return for a visit. Until then, think kindly of me."

With that, the selkie woman swam away, but she kept her word and every year, the two children could be seen swimming and playing in the water with a seal that seemed to be most familiar and all were very caring towards one another. Over the years, the Fisherman grew very lonely and sad, and could be seen wandering the shore where he had stolen the selkie's sealskin, looking out to sea as though searching for the selkie who had once been his wife.

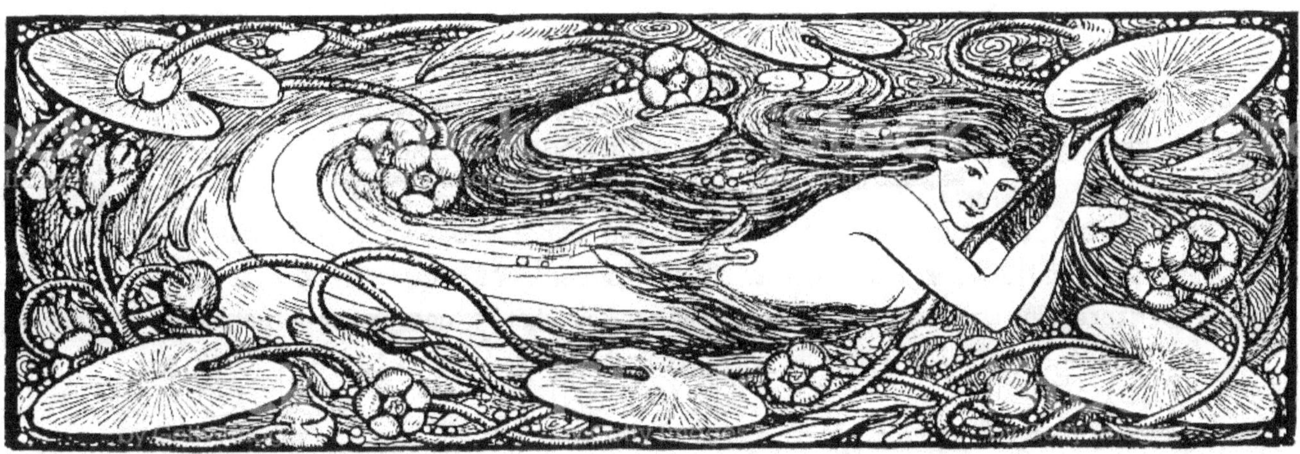

Swiss psychologist Carl Jung wrote that it is through our symbols that we can understand our psyche or soul. In the story of *The Seal Maiden* there are a number of symbols that reveal layers of meaning that can help us to successfully navigate through our own cycles of being and becoming. This is especially helpful when we are young and learning to understand what is true and has value and what does not. The most obvious symbol here is that of the sealskin which was thought to be enchanted or magical by the people of the Orkney Islands off Scotland where this myth is so prevalent

Author Clarissa Pinkola-Estes tells the story of *The Seal Maiden* in her book *Women Who Run With the Wolves*. She says that loosing one's skin, or sealskin as it's called in the story, is the same as loosing one's home and symbolizes a loss of soul because we cannot successfully sever our connection with our source without death being the ultimate result. She considers this myth to be a teaching story because it tells so clearly what can happen when one being tricks or coerces another to do something against their will and what the unhappy consequences can be.

WRITING EXERCISE: The Seal Maiden

Use the space following the writing exercises to write your responses. If you are writing your responses in a separate journal, begin by labeling a section with the name of the myth, *The Seal Maiden*, at the top of your page. Leave plenty of room in your journal to glue any quotes, images or other relevant materials you might find to add to this section.

> Write a brief synopsis of the myth, emphasizing what seems relevant to you. Then, think about a symbol that the magical sealskin might have taken in your life and describe it. This could be an attitude or attribute that protected you in dangerous situations, such as anger, shyness, or bravery.

> Write about a time when you were young and you gave your sealskin away or had it taken from you, resulting in your experiencing an undesirable consequence, or a "soul loss."

> What were the circumstances? Why and how did you suppress your natural, instinctual powers of knowing and recognizing a dangerous situation or person? What was the scariest part of that experience? Who was there to help you? What was your "key" to getting out of that situation and getting your sealskin back? What did you learn that would be valuable to share with others?

____

____

____

____

____

____

____

____

____

____

____

WRITING EXERCISE: Struggle with Identity

During our teenage years there is often a struggle to find an identity that is one's own. The following questions and statements can assist you in thinking and reflecting about your identity, then and now. Write your responses in the space below the writing exercises or write them in a separate journal.

1. Whom Did I Think I Was? Somewhere along the way, did I take on an identity that a friend or relative thought I should have or should strive to be? Whom did I think I was in my teen years? Who do I think I am now?

2. Who Am I Really? Do I have a mistaken identity---one that is not my own? Am I a "missing person" to myself? In what ways?

3. Who Could I Be? Compare "who I wanted to be when I was younger" with "who I am today." Do I carry feelings or thoughts of grief, resentment or disappointment that I could have been someone other than who I am, someone more together, richer or famous than the person who I turned out to be? How can I balance and recreate who I thought I was with what I am today and what I can become?

Here is one writer's response to writing exercises *Struggling with Identity, Who Am I Really?* and *Who Could I Be?*

STRUGGLING WITH IDENTITY

Who I Thought I Was...

I am sitting at a long table at my grandparent's home and there are relatives invited for dinner. We have finished eating the main course and my brother has been excused from the table to go play. I am the eldest grandchild, six years older than my brother, and at age 14, here I stay at the table to listen to the rambling conversations of progressive politics and wait for somebody to cut into the apple pie I keep staring at. It is 1974, post Nixon era. I try and contribute to the conversation sitting in my straight-backed chair. In the back of my mind, I see my life in my home town and the secret adventures I have been having before school, the pot-smoking rituals with friends, the getting goofy together and the expanded mind feelings which go so well with the new music I have been getting to know. I flip back to my present moment at the table and respond to questions from my elders about school and my flute playing. There are plans for my mother and I to play a piano and flute duet in the adjoining music room after dinner dishes are cleared. I maintain a façade of the good girl, more so I imagine than other girls in these types of family circumstances. I can tell because I feel lost in the role. I am wearing the mask of good girl. In this moment I don't have the means to put it all together but what has happened is this. This girl wants desperately to have the acceptance of her mother and her grandparents, especially now, after the years of dirty business with her father. No one talks to her about the incest but most of the relatives know. This girl wants to show everyone at the table how well adjusted she is; how innocent she is; and how this was maybe just a nightmare that folded quickly into the past. She smiles and gives pleasure to the elders by holding secure in the present and accountable place of the sweet eldest grandchild. Bringing the dishes in to the kitchen, she hears them talk about how well she seems to be doing. The façade feeds me enough to keep going.

Who Am I Really?

What would it have been like to get in trouble and be grounded? Where did the sassy voice get shelved? Did I really have to be so agreeable? Where did my imp go to play? In middle school years I hung out with a best friend who both loved me and teased me. She challenged me to be myself. There was one day in 8th grade that I got the idea in my head to bring an egg to school with the intent of egging a boy who had been getting under my skin and teasing me for months. Looking back at it now, he probably was just being himself and I unfairly attacked him. On the way home from school, with my raw egg intact, I threw it at his load of books underneath his arms. He was stunned and hurt. Even my friends were surprised that I really carried out such a plan. In my mind I had crushed the good girl stereotype. The pendulum swung so far over from center point that the bully jumped out of the closet. My best friend seemed to like that I tried on the bully role. I remember waking up the next morning feeling remorseful. Who was that who threw the egg? Was this the only way to find my voice? Experimenting with mean girl showed me that it wasn't necessary to go to extremes in order to feel real. Note to self: Even if I couldn't find my bold voice in those years, particularly with my mom, I did start listening to my urges and started slamming doors. She never said much about it. There were kid gloves on.

I think she didn't want to mess too much with discipline unless I really got into trouble. She felt sorry for me. She hadn't been aware of the childhood trauma taking place and when I showed it to her, she felt helpless. It reminded her of how bad things were; how beaten down she felt emotionally with my father in the early years when they were married. With her, I tempered my rebelliousness to keep the peace at home so we could have a secure and better relationship. I kept my voice down and slammed doors as my pressure release valve. She gave me freedom and I took all of it and kept secret about the brambles I got caught in.

Who Could I Be?

Could I have been someone who could have grown up with a feisty voice, rather than one who kept that voice boxed and high on a shelf? Could not the feisty voice have been accepted in the family? There was something feisty about disclosing the incest. I could have kept going in that vein and been the one to express my feelings on things that mattered to me in my world. Instead, I would seek other's words, look for people's acceptance of me and modulate my actions to match that. Up late at night, copying down poetry, wishing those words were my words; continuing to be friends with those who walked all over me. What stopped the feisty girl from rising? Shame and her need to feel loved. Shame was like a giant army boot stomping down the independent wild child. Feeling the bad child during tender years of wanting to belong made streaks of normal brashness turn into hobgoblins I wanted to banish in the closet.

As teen years rolled on, I did leave my mother's home to have my own adventures, pushed the envelope and met with some near misses on the road. The wild child was not hiding the wild so much anymore, with exception of the love for hitchhiking. The gates to the stable were gaping open. Somehow my mother must have trusted that I could take care of myself. Or, she was just distracted by the goodness of the girl. Being independent and adventurous was a salvation from dying in the valley of the meek. I devised a plan to graduate a year early and headed up to a nearby state the day after ceremonies, still wearing the cowboy boots that had poked out so boldly from underneath the graduation gown. My feistiness was in my actions. It was quite another thing though to try and speak my own mind, hold strong to my opinions, to even take a stand on things or growl with anger. These things didn't surface well for me. I noticed how easily it seemed to come to others. I had become buried inside the myth of everyone must like you so don't be displeasing. Becoming unburied has been like shedding the many scarves a gypsy dancer starts her dance with looking down to notice that I am shedding yet another one in a spiraling out of an old pattern. Some scarves I have boldly ripped off in the drive for making boundaries; other scarves are held fast to me as core identifiers. Decades turn and I am starting to notice which of the garments are those that I have worn to please people and which are mine authentically. I carry myself differently as I peel away the vestiges of the power from the inside out, but there is never a better time than now.

Anonymous
February 2017

WRITING EXERCISE: Childhood Memories

Write about a time in your childhood when you were happy. Then, write about a time in your childhood when you were very unhappy and/or afraid.

WRITING EXERCISE: Creating a "Where I'm From" Poem

This exercise is adapted from a writing template developed by Levi Romero who teaches at the University of New Mexico. Romero intended it as a writing prompt to help young people create poetry about their lives. Romero says he took his inspiration from the Kentucky poet George Ella Lyon who first wrote a poem called "Where I'm From." I adapted Romero's template and have used it many times in writing groups and it has proven to be a delightful, fun, and insightful writing experience about who we are and where we come from. Here's how it works. Read over the following template and fill in the blanks with your own information. It's that simple. And the results are always revealing and fun! Share your poem with a friend, family member or online.

Follow This Template to Write Where I'm From poem:

WHERE I'M FROM

1. I am from ________________ (An everyday item in your home, garden or on your desk)

2. From ______________ and ______________ (Objects or everyday items in your home)

3. I am from the ______________ (Description of your home)

4. ______________ (A detail about your home, such as a smell, taste, or feeling)

5. I am from the ______________ (plant, flower, something in nature)

6. The ______________ (plant, flower or tree near your home)

7. That grew in ______________ (place such as backyard, forest, desert)

8. I'm from ______________ and ______________ (a family tradition & family trait)

9. From ______________ and ______________ (family members)

10. I'm from ______________ and ______________ (family habits)

11. I'm from ______________ and ______________ (things you were told as a child)

12. And _____________ (song or saying you learned as a child)

13. I'm from _____________ (a family tradition)

14. I'm from _______ (place of birth) and _______ (family ancestry, nationality or place)

15. And _____________ (favorite family foods or meals)

16. From _____________ (short anecdote or story about a family member)

17. _____________ (Detail about the story or person)

18. _____________ (Description of family mementos, pictures or treasures)

19. _____________ (Location of mementos, i.e., under my bed, on the wall, in my heart)

20. _____________ (Add any additional description or detail)

Ana Leite Powell, a writer in a *2011 Writes of Passage class*, wrote the following poem. Her native country is Brazil.

Where I'm From

I'm from spending Christmas with the family
And not talking about our feelings
From Rosenda and Antonia
I'm from reading novels, watching movies
And from the love of travel

I am from notebooks,
From LP's and magazines
I am from the living room packed with books,
The smell of incense coming from my father's study
I am from the Atlantic Ocean,
The mango trees
That grew everywhere in my hometown

I'm from not playing outside when it rains,
Not mixing mangoes and milk
And definitely not eating hot fruit off trees
I'm from having meals together
I'm from Fortaleza and Portugal
"Torta fria" and "tapioca"*
From taking 30 minutes to say goodbye
When we leave my aunt's house

The painted tile with our family name
Bought in a souvenir shop on our family trip
To northern Portugal
That I proudly display on my dining room wall

*   Torta fria is a variation of a typical Portuguese dessert. Tapioca is how we call a type of flat bread made of tapioca starch. This was originally made by Natives in most of Brazil and was traditionally called *beiju*.

ART EXERCISE: Making a Life Map

Life Map as a Standing Folder Based on Four Rooms by Jo Bryant

This art exercise is called a *Life Map* and has proven very helpful in gaining a greater perspective about our selves and how our identity has evolved during the various cycles of growth and development. A *Life Map* is an artistic re-creation and representation that shows all the important events in a person's life. There are as many ways to create a *Life Map* as there are people, and I encourage each person to be creative as you'd like in the form you give to your map.

When I made my first *Life Map* I began with a large piece of paper and listed the significant events in my life beginning with childhood. Under each event that I listed, I drew small icons to represent the rites of passage or major events in my life that I thought were significant and had changed me in meaningful ways. It didn't take long to finish and though it wasn't especially artistic, it allowed me to see at a glance the "string" of events that had molded me into who I am today. Other class participants have used various forms for naming and placing their life events, such as a circle, a labyrinth or spiral to chart their special happenings.

Over the years I began to teach more classes on memoir writing and this exercise has become a primary core component and essential tool for writers to use in identifying what significant events in their lives they wanted to write about. If you decide you want to expand the writing you do in the *Writes of Passage* workbook, this list of significant events from your life map will be invaluable for keeping track of what you want to include in your life story.

For making a *Life Map* like the one in the photo above, you will be using a single piece of paper, folding it, then gluing photos and/or drawings onto each panel. Here are instructions for folding your paper into quarters as shown in the example. Artist and writer Jo called her *Life Map*, her house of life or Four Rooms, with its various rooms, or sections, containing photos of her and the events that filled her life.

First, begin by taking some time to decide what events you want to include on your *Life Map*. List them on a separate piece of paper or in your journal. Gather photos and other materials you want to include and decide how large you want to make the folder (again, you can refer to photo of Jo's *Life Map* to get an idea about size). You can make the beginning sheet of paper any size you choose because the finished piece will be half that tall and will have the width divided into four pages or sections.

According to Jo, you should consider the paper grain you'll be using. The paper shouldn't be too heavy, for example, or it will be difficult to fold. Large construction paper will work as will Canson's Colorline, a better quality of paper that is inexpensive and available in many colors. Black is also a great background paper as it makes photos and illustrations pop out. Here's how to fold the paper to make it into a foldout book like Jo's.

1. Fold the paper in half lengthwise with the right side out. Then, unfold.
2. Bring the short ends of the paper together and fold. Both length and width now have centerfolds. Unfold.
3. Bring the edge of one of the shorter ends of the paper to the center vertical fold and crease. Repeat with the other end of the paper.
4. Bring the wrong sides of the first fold together again and arrange so that the folder forms a Capital M with four panels when facing you. You may have to reverse the direction of some of the original folds. Now go back and re-enforce all the folds, making them as smooth as possible. Use a ruler to run along the edges to smooth and flatten them out. Your folder is now ready for decorating.
5. The first panel of the backside becomes the cover for the front four-panel folder. Use a glue stick, liberally applied, a double stick tape or a rolling tape adhesive for mounting. Avoid glue that is wet, like Elmer's, because there's a chance the paper will buckle. When you're finished attaching all materials to the folder, place wax paper between the pages to protest them, close folder and place under a couple of heavy books for a few hours or overnight to flatten.

With your completed *Life Map* as well as your other writing done to the writing exercises, you have completed the phase of youth and young adulthood and are now ready to pass onto *Phase Two* of the *Writes of Passage* journey.

PHASE TWO
Gathering Wisdom & Honoring Your Ancestors

If the only prayer you say in your whole life is
"Thank you," that would suffice.
- Meister Eckhart

Leaving Home: A Rite of Passage

Leaving the cycle of youth and entering into adulthood often means a literal leaving home. Leaving home is something most young people can hardly wait to experience. It's an exciting time because we have yearned to be out on our own and be independent for such a long time. Many young adults not only leave their homes when they go out into the world to make their way; they also leave behind or sever the values and traditions of their families, thinking them to be old-fashioned and obsolete. They want new ideas and new ways of doing things. In many ways, this is a good thing since it allows for the future to be re-created with a robustness, vitality and vision that only the young with their sense of invincibility and optimism possess. It is only much later, however, when life has dealt the young adult the numerous challenges and difficulties that are part of everyone's life, that they begin to rethink and modify their attitudes and actions. They often begin to turn again to the wisdom of their families and communities. For many, at some point in their adult cycle, they may seek to re-focus on spirituality or a deeper connection to a greater power; many find themselves turning to the values and wisdom traditions of their family and ancestors.

Adult life brings its own cycles of being and opens us to a deeper understanding of the process of life. As we grow and mature, we can sense a movement of something within us that craves time alone or seeks experiences to gain a deeper perspective on life, such as meditation, yoga, or time in nature. Each stage of life offers opportunities for growth and as we accept the natural cycles of birth and death that occur during each phase, we begin to feel an easing up of wanting to control everything in our lives, of judging ourselves and others based solely on material achievement; we begin, instead, to make room for wisdom to grow within us.

The Importance of Humor

One pathway to wisdom that has evolved for me has been to develop a sense of humor. Humor breaks up the mind's crystallizations and renders it flexible and open to new ways of seeing and experiencing life. Developing a sense of humor has helped me to identify the lighter side of most situations. While studying Shakespeare in college, one professor advised us students to look at the Fool's remarks if we wanted to understand the deeper meanings of the Bard's plays.

Various Native American tribes also have a clown or trickster that helps them laugh at themselves and keep a balanced view in life's challenging situations. I experienced this sense of humor when I took a friend to one of the Pueblo tribal dances near Albuquerque, New Mexico, during their summer dance cycle. We arrived mid-day just as the tribe's dancers were filing out from the center of the village to an underground kiva for a rest break and something to eat. Two *heyoka* as the clowns are called were standing in the middle of the plaza, dressed in clearly recognizable costumes of sash-tied skirt, no shirt and with black and white stripes painted on their bodies and topped off with a headdress that looks like two drumsticks sticking out of the top of their heads.

It is the clown's duty to entertain the crowd until the dancers return to the main plaza to resume dancing. A fact not always known by non-Indians attending a pueblo dance is that the clown's job is one of mischief-maker who can do pretty much anything they decide to do and get away with it. They love to joke, tease and otherwise embarrass the heck out of whomever they choose; and almost always the joking and teasing is sexual in nature. At the beginning of the nineteenth century, so anthropologists have written, clowns used to wear enormous dildos until various government officials and church missionaries put a stop to the clown's "indecent behavior."

From the moment my friend and I walked into the center of the plaza, the clowns began to swarm us! We kept trying to lose them by moving behind other people in the crowd, but the clowns continued to pursue us and finally, taking us by the arm, they steered us into the center of the plaza.

"It's obvious we're going to be part of the entertainment," I said, trying to reassure my friend, who was more than a little startled by having become the center of attention for the hundreds of spectators. "It's all in fun and no one's going to get hurt."

The clowns found two beach chairs, made funnier by the fact that we were both living on Maui at the time. They motioned for us to sit in the chairs and soon they began to dance around us, making gyrating motions with their pelvises. They played with my friend's long red hair causing the crowd to roar with delight. Two white women! What could be better! Then the clowns brought us each a coke to drink, followed by more dancing and gyrating pelvises. We sipped a little of the coke, not sure what else to do. I whispered to my friend that we really couldn't get up and leave until the clowns "released" us. She was taking it all in stride, however, and soon we were both laughing and enjoying the comical routine as much as the crowd.

When the ceremonial dancers emerged from the kiva to dance another round, the clowns came and stood beside us, helping us up from the beach chairs and making a low bow to each of us as we melted back into the crowd, none the worse for the experience. In fact, better for the experience because it had given us an opportunity to participate in the world belonging to another culture unlike our own and with the use of humor, had taken us in for a few moments to see life from another point of view.

Finding Wisdom From An Unlikely Source: Chaos Theory

Another source for finding wisdom that might seem unlikely but is proving richly resourceful as well as provocative comes from the field of complexity sciences. Many psychologist, futurists, and spiritual teachers are adapting principles from the fields of complexity sciences such as fractal geometry, chaos theory and quantum physics and successfully applying them to the psychology of our lives. Scientific authors John Briggs and David Peat have written a book called *Seven Life Lessons of Chaos: Spiritual Wisdom From the Science of Change* that shows specific ways chaos theory, for example, can be of help in these accelerated, constantly changing times. First, they purpose that chaos theory is evolving from a scientific theory into a new cultural metaphor. If we can regard *chaos as a metaphor*, they tell us, it allows us to query some of our most cherished assumptions and encourages us to ask fresh questions about reality. In applying a chaos metaphor to how we live our lives means "living in truth," something the authors tell us is simple, though not always easily achieved, because it requires opening ourselves up to uncertainty, discovering the edge between our individuality and what is universal, and then acting from that place.

Briggs and Peat also say that insights from chaos theory revolve around three themes: *control, creativity* and *subtlety*. Regarding control, they assure us that since all life is about uncertainty and contingencies, we must find a way to accept what chaos teaches us: that instead of resisting life's uncertainties, we should reach out and embrace them. When we do this, we summon in creativity. To live creatively, they say, requires that we give our attention to the subtle nuances and irregular occurrences going on around us. Inherent in chaos is a creativity that only emerges when we lose control and become creative participators in all that is going on. *This letting go and embracing the creative within the chaos shows us that it is in the realm of subtlety and ambiguity where real life is lived.*

Chaos theory shows us that it's exactly those tiny, insignificant things that end up playing a major role in the way things work out in our lives. An example of this can be seen in the idea of butterfly power, the seemingly insignificant flapping of a butterfly's wings that can cause a hurricane in another part of the world, that allows for the impossible to happen. It is through chaos that one person or a small group, can significantly and subtly influence the whole world.

As regards acquiring wisdom, Briggs and Peat reassure us that the emergent qualities of chaos that we could call wisdom can be compared to a system operating far from equilibrium that builds up an enormous force from our accumulated acts such as those resulting from compassion, forgiveness and so forth; once we iterate them back into the system through a process of feedback loops, an entirely new system can be created in which equilibrium once again re-establishes itself, and a new order is re-born out of the chaos that preceded it.

WRITING EXERCISE: Butterfly Power

Weather is a perfect example of a chaotic system. It is extremely sensitive to tiny influences such as temperature, wind speed or air pressure, which cycle through the system, in what mathematicians call a feedback loop. Edward Lorenz, a meteorologist who became one of the founders of chaos theory, was testing a model for predicting the weather by feeding three equations together back into one equation, creating a mathematical feedback loop. As he fed back the computations into the raw data, a process called iteration, the small initial difference between the two sets of data were quickly magnified by the feedback into a large difference. The sensitivity of non-linear systems to such tiny influences caused Lorenz to wonder if, like the old Chinese proverb, the flap of a butterfly's wings in China might cause a tornado in Oklahoma!

Because we each exert subtle influences on each other and our world, the idea of butterfly power taken from chaos theory gives us a different way to look at acquiring power and using our influence. Rosa Park's small action of remaining seated on the Montgomery bus when ordered to move to the back, was a small action that triggered a revolution, and is a good example of how butterfly power allows for the impossible to happen.

Write in the space below or in your journal about a time when you or a small group of people made a small change that may have subtly influenced the entire world. What changed and did the change that occurred seem impossible when you began?

Wisdom From Our Ancestors

There usually comes a time in our later adult lives when we experience the desire for a renewed pursuit of wisdom born out of personal loss or frustration for achieving an inner peace or a deeper meaning to life. This search or quest for a deeper understanding of the great mysteries of life often comes as a result of our confusion, fear, doubt, grief and weariness regarding the continuous struggles that life throws our way, no matter our status in life or our worthiness. While all major religions offer ways to renew and deepen faith, such as prayer, meditation and quiet reflection, it's up to us to find what path to inner wisdom works best for us. This requires careful consideration of the values and traditions from our ancestry and culture that we deem worthy of being gathered together in the deepest recesses of our heart to be cherished and given an honored place.

Seeking and sorting out values and truths that we want to cherish brings us to a greater awareness and compassion for who we are, and is known as our true "soul" work. At its core, this "soul" work requires a profound grieving and letting go. Jack Kornfield, a Buddhist teacher and psychologist from Harvard, describes meditation practice as primarily a practice of grieving and letting go. I have a good friend who works as a hospice nurse in North Carolina, who has told me many times how difficult a person's dying can be as they struggle with unprocessed grief from prior events or people in their lives. Out of grieving and letting go comes a deep healing and renewal of heart and mind that opens us up to wisdom. In the next phase of *Letting Go: Writing Through to Completions in Your Life*, we will continue to explore the healing power that forgiveness can bring to the process of grieving and letting go of people and things in our past that may have disappointed us, hurt us and no longer serve us.

Chief Seattle (Sealth) and His Legacy

The only known photo of Chief Sealth
Wiki Commons, Public Domain

In searching for ways that wisdom can inspire as well as heal, we can turn to people and cultures that have longstanding traditions of honoring the self within, of respecting the land and all its inhabitants, and who respect and care for their elders and children. One poignant example of my personal desire to remember and honor the ancestors came one afternoon when I was living on Bainbridge Island in Washington and decided to explore the area around my new island home. After winding my way through the village of Suquamish, I had just crossed the Agate Pass Bridge when I saw a sign that read "Chief Sealth's Grave." Could that be *the* Chief Seattle who spoke so eloquently of the land and his people to the white settlers who eventually took over much of this part of the NW for their own I wondered?

Since I was exploring, I decided to follow the series of yellow signs that led to a gravel driveway in back of a small church and a small graveyard. At first I didn't see any markings or signs but as I continued to walk further on, I saw to my right four tall, large black poles that were holding up two full-sized outrigger canoes, also painted black with red markings. It was a magnificent platform grave, similar to those of the Sioux and other Plains Indians. As I walked towards the platform, I followed a small paved circular pathway that completely surrounded a grave mound. At the top of the mound was a large marble headstone, marked with Chief Seattle's Indian name "Chief Sealth," and sitting on top of the headstone was a cross. Was Chief Sealth (Seattle) a Christian, I wondered? Almost covering up the cross were bones, antlers and a large moose rack someone had placed there. Bones also hung from the black poles of the canoes. Off to one side was a smaller mound with a gravestone marked, "Mary, beloved wife of Chief Sealth." Again, I wondered if his wife's name was actually that of a Christian woman, Mary, or if she was even a Native American?

I looked for a spot to sit and take in the energy of such a sacred place. The view as I looked out across the highway running directly in front of the rural churches' graveyard was an inlet of Puget Sound. I thought about what I knew about Chief Seattle. Known to virtually all environmentalists for his 1854 letter addressed to the Big Chief in Washington, in which he said he was puzzled at the White Father's request to buy the land occupied by his people. Chief Sealth wondered, *"How can you buy or sell the sky, the rain or the wind, he asks? This idea is strange to us. Every part of this earth is sacred to my people. …to us the ashes of our ancestors are sacred and their resting place is hallowed ground…Our religion is the tradition of our ancestors."*

I wondered that this gravesite behind a church should be the final resting place for the bones of such an extraordinary man and I wanted to know more. Before I left, I returned to my car to get the rare feather of a Hawaiian red-tailed sea bird that I always kept there and placed it on his grave as an act of honoring. As I turned to leave, a flock of huge ravens had congregated everywhere, leading me to imagine that they'vd also come to pay homage to this famous man who did so much to bring harmony between his people the Suquamish and the Duwamish tribes and the settlers who migrated to this region for its abundant game and fish, and for the land, which they ultimately claimed for themselves.

I decided to do more exploring of the nearby areas to see if I could find out more about Chief Sealth. Down the highway a few miles I soon found another sign, this one reading. "Individual Communal Dwelling and House of Chief Seattle." I pulled off the highway onto a gravel drive leading to a beach area. To the right was the Agate Bridge I had driven over earlier and to my left, near a small bathroom was another sign, "Old-Man House Park." Underneath the sign read: *Old-Man House served as home site, fortress and festival hall for the Suquamish Indians who once lived in this area. This structure was begun about 1800 or a little later and was added to from time to time. Over the years, thousands of Indians lived here under a single roof until they were placed on reservations. Then the great hall began to decline and little was left when the ruins burned in 1870. This was the home of Chief Seattle for many years. He was chief of the Suquamish and the Duwamish tribes that dominated the Puget Sound area. His leadership was unquestioned and his opinions were respected by all. Sealth befriended the settlers and acted frequently to promote harmony between the Indians and the pioneers."*

Shocked and tearful, my eyes returned over and over again to the passage "until they were placed on reservations."

Angry and sad, I parked my car in the parking lot near the beach where another sign identified the area as a *"sub-tidal zone: a complex living system in which all species serve a vital function; and that the largest octopus in the world lives in these waters as do the largest and fastest sea stars."*

Was this all this was left of the NW Indian tribes who lived here, I wondered? Now it was just an interesting area of marine biological diversity?

The beach rimmed the sea inlet where the Long House pits that once belonged to the Indian tribes were built. Now, raucous ravens along with numerous white people had claimed the beach as their own. As I sat down on the beach, I watched as ravens picked over the food on the deserted beach blankets left by their owners who had gone for a walk. In amazement, I watched as one ingenious raven persisted in opening a bag of chips and stealing one or two before flying off to consume its prize. A small boy showed up suddenly and exclaimed at the raven's thievery, "They took my chips. They took my chips!"

As I sat in silence watching the scene unfold, I wondered if these ravens were the descendants of ravens that had lived here during Chief Sealth's time. Were their ancestors the honored Ravens so beautifully carved on totem poles, masks, and other ritual items by the Indians who had formerly inhabited this breathtaking land?

This must be a popular beach gathering spot I thought as I watched the arrival of more families with children. I overheard one mom talking excitedly with her friend about the new brand of chocolate chip cookies she'd just bought at the store. "The kids really love them," she told her friend.

Vivid beach towels, chips, coke cans and coolers dotted the beach landscape where once Indians enacted their daily living routines and sacred rituals to honor Mother Earth and the abundant bounty of fish. What would Chief Sealth think of this scene on the beach today, I wondered.

When I arrived home, I looked up his famous 1854 speech and found this passage, *"When the last Red Man shall have perished and the memory of my tribe shall have become a myth among the White Man, these shores will swarm with the invisible dead of my tribe."*

Of course, I thought. They're still here. They're still walking the beach, making their rituals and keeping watch over the animals and the land. This thought brought me some small peace. In the months that followed, I returned to Chief Sealth's grave several times to sit quietly in honor of him and his people who lived in harmony and friendship with the land and gave us an example of a good way to live.

Totem pole on Blake Island near Seattle, Washington
overlooking the waters of Puget Sound.

Words of Wisdom From Those Who Have Influenced the World In Meaningful Ways

Thought is dualistic in nature and is regarded by many spiritual traditions as the root of all human suffering. Although thoughts and words can inspire and teach us, there can be no true healing of the mind without paying attention to the healing of the heart. Nevertheless, words can inspire us, urge us on when we've run into a wall of our own making and often, as in the case of poetry or chanting, can break us out of the mental prison we've thought our way into.

Included below are words of wisdom and inspiration from the Hopi Indians, the Dali Lama, Nelson Mandela and Mother Teresa. After reading and reflecting on these writings, there will be writing exercises to allow you to express what you think is important to you in living your life with wisdom and compassion, and what ideas and values you will use to guide yourself through your present and for some, the yet-to-come rites of passage belonging to the aging cycle. After reflecting on these words of wisdom from elders around the world, we will look to our own personal ancestry for our roots and sources of wisdom.

Wisdom from the Elders of the Hopi Nation

The Author on the Hopi Reservation

The word "Hopi" means "peace" and the Hopi Indians from the region known as the Four Corners where Arizona, Utah, Colorado and New Mexico meet, are known as the People of Peace. Their creation myth says that around 1100 A.D. Masaw, the Guardian of the Earth, gave them the way to care for the land and how to celebrate all life. For centuries they lived in peace, surviving the Spanish intrusion that lasted for 140 years and the constant depredations by Apaches and Navajos; however, at the beginning of the last century, the White government steadfastly turned the people away from Masaw's teachings by removing the village children from their homes to educate them in distant boarding schools in order "to teach them how to be civilized." Those who protested such as the revered chief Yukiuma of the Hopi village of Hotevilla, were locked up in prison. Yukiuma who was described as a gentle man, spent one year on the famous Alcatraz Island because he refused to sign a United States Government paper giving permission to remove the children. Since the Government agent and other white government officials thought the Hopi were primitive people and had nothing worthwhile to share, they never discovered the solemn vow they had given to their Creator to always follow the sacred pattern of life given to them. The "superior-minded" bureaucrats weren't interested in anything the primitives could teach them; therefore, they never discovered that the vow the Hopi had made included knowledge of certain warning signs indicating that the close of the Fourth Cycle of the world had begun; and further, that the Hopis not only possessed knowledge regarding specific warnings, but also a way of survival.

According to Hopi tradition, the Fire Clan received two small flat stones from Maasaw, who was a messenger of the Creator at the time of their re-emergence from time spent in the Fourth World. Members of the Fire Clan carried these stone tablets through their centuries of migration until they settled in the oldest living village on this continent, which they named Oraibi. These two stones, or tablets represented to the Hopi the un-relinquished aboriginal title to their land. In 1906, the Fire Clan leader, Yukiuma, in defiance of the United States Governmental policy of forced acculturation, founded a new village at Hotevilla rather than compromise the world-government relationship associated with the tablets. When Yukiuma visited President Taft in 1911 to warn of the vast destruction that would result if forced schooling of Hopi children and usurpation of Hopi land title didn't cease, he carried the tablets in a sash around his waist.

Convinced that the present state of the world allowed for no more time, Yukiuma's nephew, Martin Gashweseoma, decided to make one last attempt to set things straight. In 1990, he visited the then governor of New Mexico, Bruce King, carrying the tablets around his waist in the same fashion as his uncle had done decades earlier. Martin requested that a search be made for the original documents on which the modern claim to land title was based and offered to share the profound Hopi knowledge regarding the threat to life on earth.

The following excerpts are from a public statement that Martin released during his prophetic mission in December 1990 to the state capital at Santa Fe, which show his very dismal outlook for the future of the Hopi people and the entire planet...thoughts that seem even more relevant today:

Those who accumulate power at the expense of the native peoples think they have a God-given right, but in doing so they are increasing the threat to all life. And although they now recognize that threat, they are powerless to reverse it by any means unless they stop preying upon the native peoples. We came here to plant that seed of this realization, which could turn the course of all humanity away from disaster. An investigation within the area of the present Hopi villages would benefit all indigenous peoples. Likewise, those who now live at the expense of the native land title will be given the charge to correct their mistake, and avert the terrible consequences foreseen long ago by the Hopi, which are already in evidence today. Either way, this would benefit all humanity. Because our true original land title is essential to our role in holding this land and life in balance, we have never compromised that title by signing a treaty with the United States Government. We have never given it authority to destroy our culture and take our land, nor have the other original native peoples. Yet, this is being done here and throughout the world.

They are cutting our land into small allotments, confiscating our livestock and allowing the land to be stripped of its mineral resources. Underground water is being depleted and the land is drying up. Open pit uranium mines are polluting the area with radioactivity, causing the birth of many deformed babies. This shows what is happening to indigenous people around the world.

Those who perpetrate such abuse, and the countless modern people who thrive from it, truly have no land title. They built their power through resources taken by force, then use those resources to gain power to take even more. Since they consider the true aboriginal title of indigenous peoples to be worthless, they treat us like animals to be kicked around. But as the Purification foretold in our tradition materializes, they too will get kicked around. They will find themselves disrespected everywhere, just as they have disrespected others, and their power will collapse. Soon they will see how little power and authority they really have.

Today the American people are being taught how it feels to be held hostage. That is how we have felt, having been held hostage up to the present day. In truth, everyone in that army is held hostage by the Government. Young people who want to live a long life are forced to suffer in the Arabian Desert. We know they are about to be burnt up in a war if they don't stop. It's up to the President to recall the troops he has sent to the Middle East. They must all be allowed to refuse this fate and return home. It is especially urgent that all native people who have become involved come home right away.

As I have explained, the concept of land title based on deceit and force is nothing more than theft from the very forces that give us life. Since most of modern civilization is based on such false entitlement, it can only destroy itself. The severe problems that face not only humanity, but every form of life on Earth, serve to warn that the time of destruction is at hand. We can no longer escape. We must trace this situation to its root cause.[2]

The Hopi message has always been that of peaceful co-existence, which reflected their vow to their Creator to help preserve the inherent harmony of the world through their rituals and simple way of living. The following is a recent warning from the Hopi as well as words on how to live in a sacred way.

We Are The Ones

You have been telling the people that this is the Eleventh Hour. Now you must go back and tell the people that this is The Hour.
And there are things to be considered:
Where are you living?
What are you doing?
What are your relationships?
Are you in right relation?
Where is your water?
Know your garden.
It is time to speak your Truth.
Create your community. Be good to each other.
And do not look outside yourself for the leader.
This could be a good time!

There is a river flowing now very fast.
It is so great and swift that there are those who will be afraid.
They will try to hold onto the shore.
They will feel they are being torn apart, and they will suffer greatly.
Know the river has its destination.
The Elders say we must let go of the shore,
Push off into the middle of the river,

---

2 The Public Statement of the Keeper of the Hopi Fire Clan Tablets, Martin Gashweseoma, December 13, 1990, Santa Fe, NM, from The Planting Stick Project, Santa Fe, NM, 87505.

Mother Teresa of Calcutta, India

By Túrelio, CC BY-SA 2.0 de, commons.wikimedia.org/w/ index.php? curid=2246938

Mother Teresa was born in a small village in Albania in 1910. According to her biography, Teresa was always fascinated by stories of missionaries and their service to others and by age 12 decided to commit herself to a religious life. She often made pilgrimages to the shrine of the Black Madonna of Vitina-Letnice, a small village in Kosovo, and in 1928 she left home to join the Sisters of Loreto in Ireland to learn English, which was the language of the Sisters of Loreto in India. Once she arrived in India, she worked as a teacher at the Loreto convent school in Calcutta for twenty years until she was appointed its headmistress in 1944. She grew more and more disturbed by the poverty surrounding her in Calcutta brought on by the Bengal famine of 1943 that was followed by the violence between the Muslims and Hindu of the region during the Direct Action Day which saw rioting and mass killings occurring between the two groups.

It was during this time that Teresa says she experienced a "calling" that instructed her to leave the convent and help the poor while living among them. *"It was an order,"* she said. *"To fail would have been to break the faith."* Her biographer later wrote that it was in that moment that Sister Teresa became Mother Teresa. She soon began her missionary work with the poor, replacing her traditional Loreto habit with a simple white cotton sari with a blue border. After spending several months training in basic medical procedures, she ventured into the slums and began caring for the poor and hungry. Soon she was joined by a group of young women, who would eventually call themselves the Missionaries of Charity. Initially, their efforts were very difficult because of lack of income, food and supplies but over the years, however, their charity work expanded into creating the first hospice for the dying as well as orphanages for homeless children. By 2012, the Missionaries of Charity had over 4,500 nuns and was active in 133

---

3 No one individual has been identified as the author of these words of wisdom. Rather, they have been identified as a prophecy from the elders of the Hopi Nation.

counties, running soup kitchens, dispensaries and clinics, orphanages, schools and homes for people who were dying.

Mother Teresa received numerous honors, including the Nobel Peace Prize. Although she was canonized in 2016, she remained a controversial figure during her life and even after her death. She was both praised and criticized for her views on abortion and contraception as well as for poor conditions in her houses for the dying. Most remember her, however, for her lifelong devotion to charitable work and the help she gave to millions of people around the world. In 2017, Teresa and St. Francis Xavier were named co-patrons of the Roman Catholic Archdiocese of Calcutta.

The following words were found written on the walls of Mother Teresa's Children's Home in Calcutta, India:

People are unreasonable, illogical, and self-centered.
Love them anyway.
If you do good, people will accuse you of selfish,
 ulterior motives.
Do good anyway.
The good you do will be forgotten tomorrow.
Do good anyway.
Honesty and frankness will make you vulnerable.
Be honest and frank anyway.
What you spent years building may be destroyed overnight.
Build anyway.
Give the world the best you have
and you'll get kicked in the teeth.
Give the best you've got anyway.

His Holiness the Fourteenth Dalai Lama, Tenzin Gyatso

By I, Luca Galuzzi
CC BY-SA (reativecommons.org/
licenses/by-sa/2.5)

His Holiness the Fourteenth Dalai Lama is the spiritual leader of Tibet. He was born Tenzin Gyatso in 1935 in the small village of Taktser at the edge of the Tibetan region of Amdo. When he was around the age of two, search teams that had been sent out to locate the reincarnation of the 13th Dalai Lama declared Tenzin Gyatso to be the 14th Dalai Lama. In1950 at the early age of fifteen, he assumed his full political duties after the People's Republic of China invaded and occupied Tibet. During the 1959 Tibetan uprising, the Dalai Lama fled to India for safety where he has continued to live as a refugee. He travels the world, speaking about the welfare of Tibet, the environment, women's rights, nonviolence, interfaith dialogue, Buddhist teachings and numerous other topics.

He is a recipient of the Nobel Peace Prize and visits the West regularly to speak for ecumenism, human compassion, environmental protection and world peace. In 2006, Time magazine named him one of the "Children of Mahatma Gandhi," calling him Gandhi's spiritual heir to nonviolence.

The following thoughts are attributed to the Dalai Lama:

1. Take into account that great love and great achievements involve great risk.
2. When you lose, don't lose the lesson.
3. Follow the three R's: Respect for Self, Respect for Others, and Responsibility for all your actions.
4. Remember that not getting what you want is sometimes a wonderful stroke of luck.
5. Learn the rules so you know how to break them properly.
6. Don't let a little dispute injure a great friendship.
7. When you realize you've made a mistake, take immediate steps to correct it.
8. Spend some time alone everyday.
9. Open your arms to change, but don't let go of your values.
10. Remember that silence is sometimes the best answer.
11. Live a good, honorable life. Then when you get older and think back, you'll be able to enjoy it.
12. A loving atmosphere in your home is the foundation for your life.
13. In disagreements with loved ones, deal only with the current situation. Don't bring up the past.
14. Share your knowledge. It's a way to achieve immortality.
15. Be gentle with the earth.
16. Once a year, go someplace you've never been before.
17. Remember that the best relationship is one in which your love for each other exceeds your need for each other.
18. Judge your success by what you had to give up in order to get it.
19. Approach love and cooking with reckless abandon.

Nelson Mandela, Leader of South Africa

Nelson Mandela statue, Pretoria, South Africa By Bernard Gagnon / CC BY-SA creativecommons.org/licenses/ by-sa/4.0

Nelson Mandela, born in 1918, was a South African anti-apartheid revolutionary and political leader who became that country's first black head of state, serving as President from 1994-1999. Under his leadership, the government focused on deconstructing the legacy of apartheid brought about by long-standing institutionalized racism and through efforts to foster racial reconciliation. He was an African nationalist and socialist and earlier in his life had been the President of the African National Congress (ANC) party from 1991-1997.

While a young man, he studied law at the University of Fort Hare before working as a lawyer in Johannesburg. It was during this time that he became involved in anti-colonial and African nationalist politics. After the National

Party's white-only government established apartheid, a system of racial segregation that privileged whites, he and other members of the ANC committed themselves to its overthrow. He was influenced by the ideas of Marxism and secretly joined the banned South African Communist Party (SACP), and initially was committed to non-violent protests but with other SACP members, he co-founded a militant group that led a sabotage campaign against the government. In 1962, he was arrested, tried and convicted for seeking to overthrow the government and was sentenced to life imprisonment.

Mandela served 27 years in prison but was released in 1990 by President de Klerk when domestic and international pressure accelerated due to fears of an impending racial civil war. Mandela and de Klerk led efforts to negotiate an end to apartheid, which resulted in the 1994 multi-racial general election, bringing him and the ANC to victory. As president, Mandela led a broad coalition government to create a new constitution. In his efforts to bring the country together, Mandela sought reconciliation between the country's racial groups by creating the *Truth and Reconciliation Commission* to investigate past human rights abuses.

As we saw in the life of Mother Teresa, Mandela was a controversial figure for much of his life. Critics on the right denounced him as a communist terrorist and those on the far-left criticized him for being too eager to negotiate and reconcile with apartheid's supporters. In spite of this, Mandela gained international acclaim and recognition for his activism. Regarded as an icon of democracy and social justice, he received more than 250 honors, including the Nobel Peace Prize. In South Africa, he is held in deep respect and described as the "Father of the Nation."

Nelson Mandela's 1994 Inaugural Speech

Our deepest fear is not that we are inadequate.
Our deepest fear is that we are powerful beyond measure.
It is our Light, not our darkness that frightens us.

We ask ourselves, who am I to be brilliant, gorgeous, talented and fabulous?
Actually, who are you not to be?
You are a child of God.

Your playing small doesn't serve the world.
There's nothing enlightened about shrinking
So that other people won't feel insecure around you.

We are born to make manifest the Glory of God that is within us.
It's not just in some of us; it's in everyone.
And, as we let our own light shine,

We unconsciously give other people permission to do the same.
As we are liberated from our fears,
Our presence automatically liberates others.

WRITING EXERCISE:
Cycles of Life as Sources of Inner Strength & Wisdom

The many cycles of our life are often difficult rites of passage that present us with many challenges, such as midlife crises, divorce, illness, financial problems, unfilled ambitions and dreams. But if we can look at these challenges and difficulties with respect, we can see them in a new light; we can see them as the parts of our lives where we had the courage to face up to impossible odds; places where we showed fortitude in passing through a dark night of the soul; times when we showed amazing strength of heart when caring for others and ourselves.

In your journal or in the space below, write down any ideas, phrase or sentences that had the greatest import for you from the people mentioned and of the wisdom readings and teachings. Then, take out your Life Map that you created earlier and identify any events, or pivotal times in your life that you experienced as being the most challenging, confusing or the most difficult for you. Without overthinking it, jot down what source of inner strength or wisdom carried you through those difficult times. Remember that just as our physical life moves through its cycles, so does our spiritual life.

Wisdom From Your Ancestors & Your Roots

We often don't pay much attention to ancestors in our families until we get older and realize that soon we'll be one! Only when we focus on where we come from as we did in the poem "Where I'm From," do we realize how important it is to our identity to know who our ancestors were. Once we begin to investigate our ancestral roots, we also realize that we have uncovered and tapped into an important source of wisdom that we may not have known or believed existed.

WRITING EXERCISE: Your Ancestors & Roots

As you begin to explore who your ancestors were and where you come from, it is helpful if you know someone in your family who may have been keeping family records or has researched your family tree. Or, connecting with an older relative to ask them about the family can sometimes be a healing experience. Write about your ancestral roots by answering the following questions in your journal or on the lines that follow.

1. What are the roots of your ancestors? Celtic, Native American, African, a mixture?
    Were there any stories or myths from those traditions that influenced you or your family?
    If so, what were they?

2. Are there common themes or occupations between generations when going back in time? If so, what are they?

____

____

____

____

____

____

____

____

3. Were there strong religious or spiritual traditions that your family followed, or was that element not a part of your family life? How did the presence or absence of a religious tradition influence your early and later life?

____

____

____

____

____

____

____

____

____

4. List the one most influential member of your family, either alive or dead. They may be relatives whom you never met but whose stories are familiar to you because they were often talked about when the family got together.

____

____

____

____

5. Describe this relative by giving a few examples of distinguishing characteristics, such as, "He wanted his children to have a better life than he did and he sacrificed to ensure that this happened." Or, "She was a strong, outrageous woman who ran a saloon in a Colorado mining town." Or, "She never appreciated her family and left when her children were young, causing them enormous pain." Don't hesitate to include negative as well as positive qualities that characterized their lives.

____

____

____

____

____

____

____

____

____

____

____

6. Write a short note of gratitude to the ancestor whom you chose as being the most influential in your life, thanking them for any wisdom that has enriched your life.

7. Find a photo of your most influential ancestor and glue it into your journal or in the space below. Write a caption underneath. You may want to include a poem that you've written in their memory or other personal memento they may have given you.

PHOTO OF MY MOST INFLUENTIAL ANCESTOR

Here is an example of one writer's response to *Ancestors and Roots*:

Ancestors and Roots

Pull up a chair and get comfortable and let me recount a little story for you. The McDonald-Robertson inheritance story is so classic that every family therapist worth their salt would want to speak about it and use it as illustrative of their point about how families play out dramas in the most explicit and unconscious ways.

All my life my mother, and my father in collusion, had told me and my brothers that her mother had died when she was 7 years old. Tragic, sad, and easily dismissed family history. At age 23, arriving from Miami to Hartford, to be picked up by my father, imagine my surprise at the following exchange.

"Um, I have something to tell you."

"Ok," I said.

"Um, your mother got a letter from her mother this week."

My first thought, literally was "Oh my God, we are going to be front page news in the National Enquirer: Mother gets letter from Her Mother, from the grave."

"How is that possible?"

And there the story began to unravel. In fact, my grandmother had not died, later to be discovered that my grandfather, who my mother "adores", had committed her to a mental hospital because she was "unwell." WHAT? How was it possible for my mother to deny the life of her own mother for so many years and all with a straight face?

Ok, I could mostly swallow that and just "keep on trucking." Course the proviso in being told about the mysterious grandmother who had miraculously risen from the dead, was to not tell my brothers, which I did immediately, at the first opportunity. "Did you know that Mom's mom didn't die?"

Let me back up a little and give the context of all this, then you'll understand about the "classic family therapy" bit. I was born a McDonald, a lineage of classmen going back to the Isle of Skye in Scotland. Proud male Scotsmen, who were intellectuals and educators. Grandpa Edward-English professor and best friend to D.H. Lawrence; Great-uncle Grover-first US Ambassador to Israel; Great-Uncle Lee-beloved Dean of Students at Dartmouth College, and so on. Cripes! Wouldn't you want to be a McDonald?

Now we come to the meat of it. My father's brother, Uncle Jack, mild mannered and kind and dominated by his whiny wife Josephine, was both a Librarian and Life-Long Birder with the Audubon Society. He worked at the Library of Congress for a while and was also known for the most avidly kept Life Birder's list. Who could possibly compete with 540 species?

There's the rub my friends. What do my brothers eventually settle into in their professional lives? One a PhD ornithologist, studying birds in Costa Rica, a nod to my father's love of Latin American, and the other a Librarian, Dean of Libraries at Cornell and then in California at state supported universities. Oh the glory! Oh the accolades! Oh, the celebration of the McDonald tradition! Marvelous! Spectacular! Worthy of name-dropping at every opportunity.

Meanwhile, back at the ranch, so to speak, there is Carey Anne McDonald. Not a male, not a kilt-wearing, sword-carrying, whiskey- swigging, member of the McDonald clan. So what does she do? She investigates her mother's history of course. Southern, strange, related to Merryweather Lewis (but didn't he commit suicide?) and British---ah, the truly civilized culture of this Earth.

There was Irene, committed to a mental hospital and she was from England, by the way, and Mom was a life-long Anglophile. What the heck was that about? (Maybe another story). She later became a psychiatric nurse, helping the unfortunate who needed protection from themselves.

There was Aunt Esther, grandfather's second wife, an austere, somewhat cold, Social Worker in New York City who no one could fathom but whose work was also to provide for those "less fortunate."

Aunt Edith lived in Vermont, never married and there is a hugely mysterious story to tell about her, and all the hats from the Knox Hat Company in New York, who devoted herself to teaching children and caring for them.

Are you catching the drift of this little family history? Carey Anne eventually becomes a School Psychologist---the ultimate blending of all those, mostly hidden, women on the Robertson side of the family. How to give them a voice? How to get them the recognition they deserve? How to be their champion? How to bring into the light the shadows of the family heritage?

It has been a marriage of unconscious and conscious decisions in my life to be the carrier of those women. To provide the space and the opportunity to have their stories told, not in the minutiae of details, but in the grand scheme of being of service and petitioning to the McDonald side of the family---don't we count too?

But in this time of my transition into the role of "Wise Woman" I want to lay that burden down. I am tired, folks, of carrying the torch of understanding and healing. I have done the work of carrying those voices forward, the voices of Irene, Esther and Edith and Ellen, my mother. I want to now express the hidden talents my mother had, of genuine creativity, of passion about art and music, her appreciation and respect for all that is fine and beautiful in the world. Let me be an expression of the vision that humanity can embrace of the poignant beauty in the world without devolving into maudlin reflection or, even worse, ennui.

Thank you my family for providing the Scots courage to be a valiant soldier in the fight for what is right and the Southern/Anglican softness and vulnerability to be a true healer of wounds. And let me now, finally, come into my own and shout out my own story and truth that is free of obligation and duty. I have no clue what form that will take but am slowly hearing a whisper, an echo, a quiet shush that lets me know it is there waiting for me to claim it as my own. I am becoming free!

Carey McDonald
March 2018

WRITING & ART EXERCISE: Honoring Your Ancestors

Day of the Dead Traditional Altar
by Marianafloresocampo
CC BY-SA (creativecommons.org/licenses/by-sa/4.0)

Every area has its unique customs and traditions that shape the people who live there. In New Mexico, for example, you can see altars of various kinds belonging to many spiritual traditions. Native Americans will often keep objects sacred to their ancestors in special places in their homes or in their ceremonial chambers called kivas to honor their relatives who have passed. Hispanic people, who celebrate the *Day of the Dead* every year, also build niches as places of special honor in their homes and churches to hold photos of an ancestor or statues of a saint or The Virgin Mary known as Our Lady of Guadalupe. These special places are set aside as a reminder of their dead relatives or to indicate the presence of a saint or other holy person.

> In this art exercise you will create an altar or special place for your ancestors. It can be as simple as a space on your bookshelf, or a separate table or chest. Place as many photos of ancestors most influential in your life on the altar as you wish. Place any sacred objects that belonged to them or that remind you of them. Decide what other ways you will honor your ancestors, such as with prayers, blessings, burning incense, a candle or other rituals that you create to invoke their presence in your life.

> In this writing exercise, write a few paragraphs in which you identify the relatives in the photos you placed in a special place or altar in your home. Tell something about them and how they were special to you. Describe how creating an altar to honor your ancestors impacted you or what you experienced in doing this exercise.

PHASE THREE
Letting Go: Writing Through to Completions in Your Life

"Cheshire-Puss," she began, "which way should I go from here?"

"That depends a good deal on where you want to get to."

"I don't much care where…" said Alice.

"Then it doesn't matter which way you go," said the Cat.

"…So long as I get somewhere."

"Oh, you're sure to do that," said the Cat, "if you only walk long enough.

In that direction lives a Hatter, and in that direction lives a March Hare. They're both mad."

"But I don't want to go among mad people," Alice remarked.

"Oh, you can't help that," said the Cat.

… From Alice In Wonderland by Lewis Carol

The third phase of *Writes of Passage: Writing Through the Seasons of Your Life* brings you to the part of your journey quest where we actively engage in the process of letting go in order to release or bring to completion anything or anyone that might be holding you back from living a happy, meaningful life. In this particular section, *Letting Go: Writing Through to Completions in Your Life,* we will look at any unfinished business that keeps you from walking fully in your wholeness as an integrated person living in the power of now.

Just like Alice in the quote above, we often share the feeling of not wanting to "go among mad people," and if we must, which the Cat says we can't help but do this, then how do we remove the "mad people"in our lives? The following exercises are a few examples that will help you and give clarity as to how you can turn these situations around.

Learning From a Petty Tyrant

Carlos Castaneda was an American author who graduated from the University of California with a PhD in Anthropology. Beginning in 1968 and ending in 1998, he wrote a series of books that described his shamanic training and experiences with characters in his books called Don Juan and Genaro Flores. In his book *The Fire Within*, Castaneda's teacher the shaman Don Juan tells him he should be grateful for the constant insults that another warrior-shaman named la Gordo is always hurling at him.

"She is your petty tyrant," Don Juan tells Castaneda.
"What is a petty tyrant?" Castaneda asks.

Don Juan tells him that a petty tyrant is a tormentor, someone who either holds the power of life and death over you or simply annoys you to the point of distraction. According to Don Juan, a petty tyrant is actually helpful and is someone we can't do without because they provide ways for a warrior-shaman to lose their self-importance and become a more balanced person, strong but also humble.

WRITING EXERCISE: Petty Tyrant

Think about someone who has functioned as a Petty Tyrant in your life. Write a letter to this Petty Tyrant, who may be dead or alive, thanking them for whatever they did to you that helped you to become a stronger and wiser person. By writing this letter, whether you ever show it to them or not, you are demonstrating that they no longer have any power over you and that you have let them and the former situation go.

____

____

____

____

____

____

Here are two examples of writing done by former *Writes of Passage* participants to the writing exercise of Petty Tyrant.

Petty Tyrant

As I sit here contemplating my assignment, I'm wondering why I'm having a hard time with this one. The tyrant out my window is the wind that keeps distracting me from my task at hand. It is gusting 25 to 30 mph at least and reeking havoc with my yard. Watering cans are blowing all over the place; the cloth sunscreen on the portal is straining to rip from the staples holding it in place. Something has come loose and is flapping madly. The trees are swaying like some madman or head banger at a metal concert. Crazy. Crazy. The nature of wind as a petty tyrant, pushing and pushing at us unrelenting until we either snap or learn to bend like bamboo and allow the wind to wash over us. Once the gust takes a pause, the ever so subtle cessation in the chaos, we can pick our head up for a moment and observe. We must learn to bend or we will snap under the constant badgering. I guess that's what the trials of our life are like. Each and every petty tyrant I have encountered through this life has helped to temper me like a metal sword. Each has honed my edges to be razor sharp to cut through the bull shit and get to what is really important. Like the unrelenting gusts of wind teaching us that to resist and be so rigid will cause harm to ourselves. We must know when to bend, how much to bend so we can bounce back up and continue to grow. That's what I get as I watch the trees and grasses outside my window.

I think my dad was a petty tyrant in my life. He was always on us. He was the wind of my childhood and for a while it was I who didn't bend but resisted and rebeled. I was finding myself and testing out my wings. I took some rough tumbles as my wings bent and broke as I learned to ride the current. I had many tyrants as I look back on my life…nuns, teacher, friends, girl friends, bosses and too many to write about each one separately. I realize the lessons were similar and that I had to be forged in all those fires in order to come out stronger and stronger each time. I'm grateful to all those that served this purpose in my life. I would not be the person I am without the tempering. I have accomplished so much and could not have been in my acupuncture practice for almost 30 years. I have been able to be present for my clients; I have been faced with so many things that I didn't know about and because I know how to learn and explore, I have been able to guide people in their quest for wellness. I am a funning, engaging, compassionate person because of the tyrants. I'm strong and competent. Thank you to the blacksmiths that forged me.

Dairne McLoughlin
March 2018

Petty Tyrant

Lisa found her way to me very quickly at the start of my sophomore year of high school. We were both enrolled in the small alternative school program within the high school. She was a year older than me and due to a dysfunctional family, at age sixteen, she was off living on her own at other people's houses. We soon became very close and it was a welcome change, as most of my middle school years I had spent longing to be popular. I had a few close friends but with them I sometimes felt as if I was from a different planet.

Lisa was exotic in her dress and in her stories of life. She would go to thrift stores in Cambridge near Harvard Square and bring to my room the outfits she had found; scarves and shirts decked with mirrors and embroidery. She would change clothes in front of me without batting an eye and would toss her head back and ask me what I thought. She acted as if she had grown up in the theater. She had a certain sexy way about her and an air of bravado, often boasting about how many men had been attracted to her. This is what real men like in a woman, she would say, as if trying to teach me. Over the years I heard about all the breakups she had had and how most men couldn't handle her because, she'd say, "I wasn't going to stand for being their mother or play into the Madonna complex."

In a particularly desperate time when Lisa had been tossed out of one house, she appealed to my mother to be housed in our attic spare room. It was the end of my last year of high school and my mother listened to my appeals as well. Lisa moved in and I gained a wild sister. We had developed some tender aspects of our relationship over the time we had known each other. She would play guitar and we would sing together, harmonizing on Crosby, Stills, Nash, & Young songs and on her own creations as well. I learned Transcendental Meditation and together we would meditate back to back before dinner. We would put on feminist music, like Chris Williamson and dance around my room. She took me out to join sacred dance circles, the Dances of Universal Peace, in Cambridge and Boston. Through Lisa, I met people my parent's age who were in another category of cool. I would watch Lisa interact with other people and wonder about her magnetism.

I remember the cards she would write me for no special occasion. Her handwriting was slanted toward the right and would cover the entire card. I could tell it was written very fast, gushing like the way she would tell stories. She would tell me about how amazing I was and how much like an angel I was and how innocent and pure and full of light. At first I was stunned. I had never quite known how to take compliments.

Over time something started spoiling the magic. I noticed that Lisa started becoming jealous of friends I was making, saying that before I had met her I hardly had any friends. I am the one who introduced you to all these people, she would say, and you were meek. There was a male musician friend she had introduced me to who became my boyfriend for a while. He told me that Lisa was constantly putting me down behind my back. I noticed that after giving me cards of appreciation or when giving me verbal compliments that she would point out that I had a certain smile that was too proud, that was more like a sneer. She told me that I came across humble around people but that secretly I really was conceited and saw myself as above others. Lisa had been the alpha wolf in our relationship and I didn't know what to say to defend myself from these accusations. I went from being in awe of her to feeling confused about who I was encountering from day to day, friend or foe? When I went away to Goddard College, she came to visit me and settled into the community. She quickly became connected to interesting people and this time it was me who started feeling jealous. I had been there an entire year and she only a month and she would introduce me to people I had wanted to become friends with *but was too shy to reach out. Then she would talk about me to these same friends in ways I heard about later as being disrespectful, all the while reaching out for my continued friendship.*

We drifted apart some but there was one place we would always meet up, in the presence of our mutual elder friend, healer and herbalist Adele Dawson. Adele had a very open and receiving personality, quiet yet powerful and she was able to handle Lisa's energy and dissipate the scorpion sting, even when it was directed straight at me in the public communal setting of the farmhouse kitchen. Adele provided one of the only neutral zones I felt safe in around Lisa. More trouble was around the corner though. There was a young man whom I had a particularly special relationship with who worked as gardener for Adele. He and I would play flutes in the woods together and talk a blue streak about the magical mystical occurrences in our lives. I longed to be intimate with him but he saw me more as a younger sister, a confidante, but not a lover. He met Lisa and her magnetism took over. I had to cover my ears when she would talk about their trysts together. Then he would ask me why I didn't get along with Lisa. That was the tipping point. My blood was starting to boil with the anguish of having been befriended by her only to be punched on and walked over repeatedly. What was my lesson here?

Lisa had become the petty tyrant in my life. She showed me that I needed to find my own dignity, to stand my own ground and to accept who I was from within. The longing for a deep connection with a female friend had overshadowed any awareness of the pit of vipers she provided in the drama of our relationship. By my mid-twenties, I had finally come to a certain impasse with her and I told her that I could no longer be friends with her. In that same year, I also left a verbally abusive relationship with an older man I had moved in with. Maybe it was the moment when the two of them were fighting about me in my presence that I decided to take the cap off the boiler. I returned to my center. I claimed some self-respect and took account that ultimately, I would be a much better friend to someone by cheering for the home team first. I thank Lisa for the opportunity to have learned that.

Rebecca Leeman
March 2018

What Are Crazymakers & How Can We Get Rid of Them?

Artist and author Julia Cameron says in her book *The Artist's Way* that creative people often involve themselves with people she calls *crazymakers*. She defines *crazymakers* as people who constantly create storm centers around themselves. These people can be charismatic, she says, but are often out of control and addicted to drama. Cameron warns that *crazymakers* can take over your entire life and are especially destructive for the creative person, and those who like to help others get their lives together, often called *enablers*. *Crazymakers* are driven by their need for power and drain others to get it, she says. Cameron makes the startling observation that creative people will put up with the chaos of a *crazymaker* because they find it less threatening than the challenge of attending to their own creative lives! She says creative people often will use a *crazymaker* to block their own creative flow.

WRITING EXERCISE: Crazymakers

Think for a moment and see if you can identify anyone in your life who fits Cameron's description of a *crazymaker*.

Write a letter or poem to this *crazymaker* in your journal or the space below. Tell them all the things you've wanted to say to them for a long time but haven't been able to say or were afraid to say.

____

____

____

____

____

____

____

____

____

After you've finished writing your letter, take a few quiet moments to reflect and identify any ways that you might be avoiding your own creative flow by allowing the crazymaker to stay in your life, such as never finding the time to attend to your own creative projects or efforts; or listening to your inner critic who assures you that you have nothing of importance to say; or of succumbing to the idea that you can "save" this person who only needs a caring person to listen to them.

____

____

____

____

____

____

Conclude this exercise by imagining concrete ways to correct any negative self-talk and avoidance behaviors you have, such as making a commitment to write or paint every day or three times a week at a scheduled time and then sticking to it. Enter those times in your day planner as though it were an appointment you've made, because it is! Then, show up and do what you've committed to do! You will begin to feel a sense of renewed power as you take control over your own life, by taking these step-by-step measures and holding firmly to them.

____

____

____

____

____

____

____

Here is an example of writing to a *Crazymaker* in your life:

Crazymaker

You blew into town with your guitar.
We met at a community open mic.
You said you had talent most other people didn't
---that you could see people's musical parts in your head.

You asked me to join a band with another singer.
We still had to find that other singer.
When we were three, we rehearsed on your terms.
Here is your part. Here are the songs. Oh, and we need a car to go to gigs.
Here, Becky, is a car you should buy. It's only 300 dollars and we can pay you
back from the money we will earn with gigs.

You weren't even that cute.
It must have been the music and the harmony together.
Initially, you were impressive.
Then, you became tiresome.

We had one gig at a sleepy bar in the working class town nearby.
The bouncers there already had an attitude about you.
Even at 21, I should have seen you were trouble.

I did have fun singing with the other woman.
We would roll our eyes at you when you weren't looking.
The car was a junker.
I don't remember it ever being registered.

The music together got a little better.
I let you wear my precious jean jacket
The one that I had carefully embroidered with rock & roll music lyrics and artists across
every inch of the garment

You told me I had a great voice
And that we blended like warm milk and honey together.
You taught me how to make friends with the mic.

I fronted you more money so we could buy me a better microphone.
There was never another gig, nor another piece of equipment.

Forgiveness

Forgiveness is a necessary first step in the process of grieving and letting go of people and things from our past that have caused us grief and heartache. Psychologists, counselors, and people from diverse spiritual traditions teach that forgiveness is an essential step in coming to completion in a positive way with hurtful people and things from our past. Forgiveness is done for the primary benefit of ourselves, not for the other person whom we, nevertheless, may see as having been at fault. We forgive others in order to release the powerful emotions of sorrow, anger, resentment and loss we carry around like a large sack full of burdens we have strapped to our backs and we need to put down. When we forgive a person or painful event in our lives, we put our burdens and negativity down, and as we do this, we open up a space in our hearts and minds for an awareness to grow that our pain is a shared pain; we come to the realization that everybody experiences pain in their lives. It is part of the human experience and once we recognize this, we feel a deep connection with each other. We learn that we must open our hearts to all of life, to the pain as well as the pleasure. This acceptance of the dualistic nature of life results in a wisdom of the soul through which we can create a greater and more authentic identity for ourselves—one that is rooted in the heart.

By Elizabeth Prosapio

WRITING EXERCISE: A LETTER OF FORGIVENESS

Write a letter to a parent, friend, partner, child, or co-worker asking forgiveness for something you've done or forgiving them for something they've done to you. Or, you may want to write your letter on stationery and address an envelope with the person's name on the outside and put it in a special place for safekeeping. One day you may return to find and read this letter with a great deal of surprise and/ or empathy for how deep your wounding was from this experience. Perhaps you'll be able to see how writing this letter helped to release the burden you were carrying for that person or event.

Here are two examples of beautifully written letters of forgiveness by former writers in a *Writes of Passage* class:

Forgiveness

I forgive you for years of not knowing what the hell was happening to me in those secluded cabins in the woods at the hands of my own father.

I forgive you for disappearing in the back room when it was time for him to pick us kids up for weekends and you not being able to see the dread or confusion and numbness in my expression when he came to the door.

I forgive you for not picking up on the hints about being too ill to go. His presence at the door made you too ill to be accounted for yourself. I get it now, that he forced himself on you when you were 17. I was born from that trauma and I knew to grow butterfly wings.

I understand that by the time my brother was conceived, there had been six years of unhappy marriage, of infidelities and cruel taunting about other women and his attitude about you being cold and prudish. I would hear this from him about you during my own trauma years with him. If I had been your own mama back in high school, I would have watched you like a hawk. If I had been your ideal mama, I would have held you and snuggled you and supported your strength as a young woman.

When truth was out and it was more horrible than you could imagine, I forgive you for not putting down your white heat anger long enough to soften and fold me into your arms and tell me it was going to be OK.

I forgive you for not knowing that what I needed most from you was to show me safe affection. I forgive you for not knowing that drawing me out and talking to me more about who was to blame could have helped me not feel so much shame. In those days, kids weren't part of adult conversations like this. You were hurting and downtrodden and I know you blamed yourself for what happened even though we both know that we can't stop all the sickness in the world, even when it lands at our doorstep.

I forgive you for not being the mama lion when I needed you most.

I know what that is like now.

In this moment I give you space in my life to show me your lion. I honor her.

And I will sit with you, even if only in dreams, woman to woman, with your own trauma to bear witness to the transformation and healing within your experience.

I love you,
Your daughter

Anonymous
2015

Here is a second letter of forgiveness, which as you can see, has a very special recipient.

Forgiveness

Dear Carey Anne,

Well, girlfriend, you need a letter of forgiveness for yourself to be part of this journey of healing you be on. I want to help you forgive darlin' cuz being in a place of shame and doubt ain't helping you atall, atall!

So, let's just begin this little song and dance with first things first. You spent a whole lotta' dough on them folks and you know it weren't worthwhile, but you did it anyway. And we can be stuck in some ugly place of self-recrimination or we can understand that whole episode for what it was: You were in major grief honey, and you didn't have your head on straight. And them people wanted to take advantage like nobody's business. Especially that bloodsucker woman; you know a bloodsucker is a vampire and that was what she was honey child. Just a plain ole' vampire and you got sucked on and suckered. No sense staying stuck in that mud pit and worrying and fretting your pretty little head about all that money. It done gone and there ain't nothing you can do about it but say goodbye and be grateful they didn't rob you of all of it.

Now the other features of this story were a little more subtle and hidden like. The man of the story was all you could have hoped for in a lover and a boyfriend: handsome, talented, funny, smart as a whip, and a true charmer. He has some sexy vibe comin' off of him that is enough to make you break out into a sweat. Oooweey! Honey, I need a glass of ice water just thinking about it. So give yourself a pass on that one and realize that you were hurtin' and so ready for some down home lovin' and he just fit the bill (except of course, for the fact that the woman vampire was there in the situation doin' her blood sucking thing). And if truth be told, he got a little vampire in him too, or maybe more to the point, he got a big chip on his shoulder about how the world owes him and you came along to just scratch that itch.

Inside of you, you got a big heart and a tendency to live in full denial of reality. Fantasy life is good, don't get me wrong, but sweet pea, it be time to grow up and leave them childish ways behind. You be smart enough to see the reality of situations and make them grown up decisions about what be good for you. And that kina' mess you were in, no matter how sweet feeling some of the times may have been, ain't good for you and you know it. So the way to forgive yourself for that little detour in your life is to say and truly KNOW that you won't ever let yourself be suckered like that again by anyone else. It just ain't gonna happen and that's the end of that story. You got that? It ain't never gonna happen again.

It be time to move along the path of inspiration, sweetness. You got a lot of talents and God-given gifts to share with the world and you better get crackin'. That jewelry you make, that journaling and drawing thing, that writing you be doin', the new chance you be takin' to try new things. You to be admired for all that creative force in you and it be time to move forward in your life and share them gifts. And even better, you also be thinking about movin' part-time to some place tropical-like and warm. You know that is the best thing for your spirit. Warm breezes done always made you smile.

Finally honey child, you be kind to yourself. You were just temporarily out of your mind and need to be forgiven that craziness. What other choice do you have? Stay stuck in the pit of self-pity? No, thank you God. That be a really big mistake to waste your time and energy on that shit. You be lovable and creative, and funny as anything, and it be a ripe time to embrace all of that positive-ness.

With love, Your Paulina

Carey McDonald
March 2019

GUIDED VISUALIZATION: Butterfly Woman

We are going to take a healing journey to a beautiful forest. We'll begin our journey by taking a few deep breaths, letting the healing rays of light that stream through the rooftop of the forest cover us. Feel yourself relaxing, as you walk deeper into the forest. Immediately you see a large bear standing directly on the path in front of you. She is a Spirit Bear. She silently communicates to you that there is nothing to fear. As soon as you relax, she walks up and wraps her strong arms around you and gives you a gentle bear hug for a long time while you feel yourself releasing all the pent-up emotions you are carrying. Feeling even more relaxed, you thank the Spirit Bear and continue your walk into the dense forest.

In the distance you see a deer stag and a doe. They beckon you to follow them. They tell you they have something to show you, something that they have made especially for you. As you follow the stag and doe further into the forest, you feel yourself falling into a deeper state of relaxation and comfort. The two deer stop and point to a group of other deer that seem to be waiting for you. All the deer are standing in a circle around a nest of feathers and soft leaves, which they have made for you. They motion for you to lay down and rest for a while. The deer stand silently over you, sending you healing energy as you nestle among the soft feathers of the nest. Your heart is filled with love at this unexpected gift and you feel a profound peace and rest filling your entire body and mind.

After some time has passed, the deer tell you they want to take you to meet a very special couple, Dr. & Ms. Heart, two elves who live in the hollow trunk of a tree. It seems Dr. & Ms. Heart have also prepared something special for you. Standing in front of a small door carved out of the tree trunk, Dr. & Ms. Heart greet you warmly with hugs and invite you inside. You enter their small home and as you sip the sweet tasting tea they offer you, they tell you that they have been waiting for your visit for a very long time. They tell you they know you have come for a healing of your heart. They invite you to lay down on a bed underneath diamond-shaped windows where brilliant yellow and rose-colored light streams down on you. They tell you how beautiful you are. How like a butterfly you are, beautiful, tender, and delicate; how you are a symbol of wondrous transformation.

You take a few deep breaths as you take in all their healing words and energies. Suddenly cocoons cover your entire body and from them hundreds and hundreds of beautiful butterflies burst out of you. They cover the walls, the ceiling, the tables and floors. There are thousands of them in every conceivable color and iridescence. You realize in a brilliant flash of insight that you have been transformed into BUTTERFLY WOMAN. You are able to see that every room of your own home outside the forest is also being filled up with beautiful butterflies. As you soak up the truth of being BUTTERFLY WOMAN, you hear Dr. & Ms. Heart telling you that you can come back to visit them anytime, suggesting you do so regularly. You get up from the bed and thank them, promising to return very soon.

Take a few moments and come back to the present reality of your room. When you're ready, write about your experience in the space below and how you feel now as BUTTERFLY WOMAN.

____

____

____

____

____

____

____

____

____

____

____

____

VISUALIZATION: Accepting Gifts of Healing and Peace

Have your journal close at hand as you will write in it after your meditation. You can read this visualization into a tape recorder and play it back, or you can read over the text, remembering the important parts and then take the journey through your active visualization.

Close your eyes and take a few deep breaths, letting yourself relax. Let go of all thoughts of your day, your job, your life and focus on this moment. See yourself going to a favorite place where you always feel happy and calm. Notice as many details about the place as possible: Is it cold or hot? Is it in the woods, a mountaintop, beside the ocean? Take a seat in a comfortable place and allow yourself to take everything in, enjoying the peace and serenity that you feel when you're there. Bring your attention to a part of your body where you are carrying some sorrow or deep wound. Let yourself feel into that area with tenderness. You may want to place your hand over that area. As you take a few more deep breaths, you notice that you are not alone. Someone is approaching you. You recognize them as someone who has come to help you heal the wound you have been carrying; someone who will give you something that will open your heart in a new, unexpected way.

Allow your heart to open to receive whatever it is that this special being has brought to you. Ask the guide to sit with you for a while. Ask if they have anything they want to tell you. Focus on the energy behind their words. As the guide turns to leave, thank them for the gifts and insights they have given you.

Thank the place itself before you take your leave. As you slowly open your eyes, you find yourself back in this present reality. Wiggle your hands and toes; straighten your shoulders. When you are ready, take out your pen and write about your experience.

____

____

____

PHASE FOUR
Finding The Soul of Your Work:
Writing Past Fear to Your Passion

It's not the agony of the quest
but the rapture of the revelation
... Joseph Campbell

Psychologist James Hillman, author of *The Soul's Code: In Search of Character and Calling*, tells us that there is something beyond the either/or category of genetics and environment in developing character. He believes that there is a guiding force at work in each person's life, which he calls the *daimon*, a word from the early Greek philosopher Plato. Christians later referred to this guiding force as a guardian angel while many people today refer to it as spirit guide or lightforce. Hillman developed what he called an "acorn theory" to explain how a blueprint for human beings develops. Just as the magnificent oak tree's destiny is written in the tiny acorn, humans, too, have a particular image that forms the essence of their life, or destiny, that asks to be lived and is already present in us when we are born. Hillman urges that we look at every aspect of what makes up our lives, from our childhood impulses, fantasies, and ideas, even to our accidents, as sources that offer clues into what our individual daimon demands of us in order to fulfill our destiny.

Hillman rejects the idea that it is only the traumatic experiences of our early years that shape our personalities and development. *He proposes that our lives may be determined less by our childhood than by the way we have learned to imagine our childhoods.* Rather than focus on how our childhood may have twisted and damaged us, he suggests that we look at what else was there in our nature. In this way, we can bring back any feelings we had in our early years regarding our destiny. What must be recovered, Hillman insists, is a sense of personal calling, the real reason for our being alive. Our true biography, or destiny, has already been written into our individual acorn but is stolen from us by the many psychological frameworks that shape our lives to fit neatly into stages of an already planned life map, starting with childhood, a troubled adolescence, to midlife crises, and onto aging and finally, death. He says that it is not so much repression of our past as it is repression of our acorn and the past mistakes that we have made in our relation to it.

Overcoming Fear: The Story of Jumping Mouse

The following is an adaptation of *The Story of the Jumping Mouse* from a book called *Seven Arrows* by Native American author Hyemeyohsts Storm. Storm tells the story through the experiences of a small mouse that goes on a journey to find out what the roaring in his ears is and where it is coming from. In the process of his journey into the unknown that requires he move past his constant fear, the small creature is transformed into a powerful being: his once dreaded enemy, the Eagle.

Once there was a Little Mouse. Like all mice, he was very busy with mice things, and spent his days searching and constantly touching his whiskers to the grass. But once in a while he would lift his head, wiggle his whiskers and wonder about things. One day he scurried up to a fellow Mouse and asked him, "Do you hear a roaring in your ears, my brother?"

"No, no" answered the other Mouse, not even lifting his busy nose from the ground. "I don't hear anything. I'm busy now so talk to me later."

When Little Mouse asked another Mouse the same question, he only stared hard and told him he was foolish in the head. Little Mouse shrugged his whiskers and busied himself again, determined to forget the whole thing. Still, he kept hearing the roaring and even though it was very faint, one day he set out to investigate where the sound was coming from, leaving his busy mice friends behind. He had only gone a little way when suddenly someone said hello.

"Hello, little brother," the voice said, causing Little Mouse to practically jump right out of his skin. "It is I, Brother Raccoon. What are you doing here all by yourself?"

Timidly Little Mouse replied, "I hear a roaring in my ears and I've come to investigate."

"That roaring you hear little brother is the River," said the Raccoon.

"What is a River?" asked Little Mouse curiously.

"Walk with me and I'll show you," Raccoon said.

Little Mouse's heart was pounding hard as he walked with Raccoon on strange paths he'd never been on before. He smelled the scent of many things that had happened on the path before and was so frightened that he almost turned back many times.

76

Soon they arrived at the River. The River roared, sang, cried and thundered as it made its way downstream and Little Mouse was able to see little pieces of the world being carried along on its surface.

"The River is so powerful!" Little Mouse exclaimed.

"Yes, it is a great thing," agreed Raccoon. "I have to go now but before I do, let me introduce you to a friend who will take good care of you."

Raccoon pointed to a Frog sitting on a bright green lily pad. "Hello, Little Brother," said the Frog. "Welcome to the River."

Little Mouse turned to Frog and asked him if he was afraid of being so far out in the great River.

"No," answered the Frog. "I'm not afraid because I'm the Keeper of the Water. At birth I was given the gift to live both above and within the River. You can't see me when ole Winter Man comes and freezes the River's Medicine but I am here below. To visit me, you must come when the world is green. Would you like to have some Medicine Power?" Frog asked Little Mouse.

"Me? Medicine power? Yes, if it is possible."

"First, crouch as low as you can and then jump as high as you are able. Then you will have your Medicine."

Little Mouse jumped as high as he could and couldn't believe what his eyes saw: the Sacred Mountains. In an instant, he fell back to earth and landed in the River. Frightened, he scrambled back to the bank as quickly as possible.

"You tricked me," he yelled at Frog.

"Oh, you're not hurt, Little Mouse. Don't let your anger and fear blind you. Tell me, what did you see?"

"I saw the Sacred Mountains," Little Mouse said.

"Now you will have a new name," Frog said. "Jumping Mouse!"

Little Mouse was thrilled with his new name, Jumping Mouse. "Now I must go back to my people and tell them of my adventures," he said as he left Frog and the great River.

When Jumping Mouse returned to the world of mice, no one believed what he had done and seen. For one thing, he was wet and there had been no rain, and try as he might, he could find no way to explain to them about the River. The mice people were afraid of him and even though Jumping Mouse stayed with them, he couldn't forget his sight of the Sacred Mountains and soon determined to return.

He scurried to the edge of the mice world where he looked out onto the great Prairie. As he looked up into the sky, he saw it was full of dark spots, each one an Eagle. But he gathered his courage and in spite of his pounding heart and the dark spots in the sky, he ran as fast as he could out onto the Prairie.

When he came to a large patch of sage, he paused to catch his breath. An Old Mouse was there and welcomed him.

"Such a wonderful place with plenty of seeds and nesting material and so many things to be busy with," Jumping Mouse said in amazement.

"Yes, this is a wonderful place. You can see all the beings of the Prairie; the Buffalo, Antelope, Rabbit and Coyote."

"Can you also see the River and the Great Mountains?" Jumping Mouse asked him.

"I know there is a Great River but I'm afraid the Great Mountains are only a myth. You should forget your passion to see them and stay here with me. Everything you could possibly want is here and it is a good place to be."

Jumping Mouse was astonished that anyone could say such a thing about the Medicine of the Sacred Mountains. He thanked Old Mouse for the meal. "I am going to seek the Sacred Mountains and must leave now."

"You're a foolish mouse," Old Mouse told him. "Look up in the sky. All those spots are Eagles that will catch you if you leave here."

But Jumping Mouse was determined. He arched his tail and ran as fast as he could until he ran into a stand of chokecherries where it was cool. There was water and seeds to eat and many other busy things to do. He was investigating his new habitat, when he heard heavy breathing. It was a Great Buffalo lying before him.

"Hello, my Brother," said the Buffalo.

"Hello, Great Buffalo," said Jumping Mouse. "Why are you lying here?"

"Because I am sick and dying," the Buffalo said, "and my Medicine told me that unless I receive the eye of a mouse, I cannot be healed. But there is no such thing as a mouse."

Jumping Mouse was shocked. I have two eyes, he thought to himself. Does the Great Buffalo want one of my eyes? Not sure what would happen, he scurried back into the shelter of the chokecherries. Soon the Buffalo's breathing became harder and slower.

He will die if I don't give him one of my eyes, Jumping Mouse thought. Then he made a decision.

"You're a great being. I have two eyes and I will give you one of them." The moment he said those words, one of his eyes flew from his head and the Buffalo was made whole again.

"Thank you little Brother," the Buffalo said. "I know of your quest to visit the Sacred Mountains and your visit to the River. You have given me back my life and now I will help you by taking you to the foot of the Sacred Mountains. All you need to do is run underneath me and the Eagles won't be able to see you."

Once they had reached the Sacred Mountains, the Great Buffalo stopped. "This is where I must leave you," he said.

"Thank you for your help," Jumping Mouse replied. "Running with only one eye was hard and I was very afraid of your earth-shaking hooves."

"You had no need to fear because my way of walking is the Sun Dance Way and I always know exactly where my hooves will land. I must return to the Prairie and my people now but you can always find me there."

As Jumping Mouse began to investigate his new surroundings, he saw a Gray Wolf sitting nearby, doing absolutely nothing. "Hello Brother Wolf," Jumping Mouse called out.

"Yes, yes. That is what I am. I am a Wolf," said the Wolf, but almost immediately his eyes dimmed and he became silent again, completely without memory of who he was. Every time Jumping Mouse would remind him that he was a Wolf, he would get excited but then the next moment, he would forget again.

Jumping Mouse went to the center of the new place and listened hard for a long time to the beating of his heart, trying to understand what he should do. Soon, he made up his mind and scurried back to the Wolf.

"Brother Wolf, I know what will heal you. It is one of my eyes. You are a greater being than myself and I am only a Mouse. So please take it."

As before with the Buffalo, when Jumping Mouse spoke these words, his other eye flew out of his head and the Wolf, like the Buffalo, was healed.

Tears of joy fell down the cheeks of Wolf but Jumping Mouse couldn't see them because now he was completely blind.

"Thank you Jumping Mouse," said the Wolf. "You are truly a great being. Now that I have my memory back, I will be your guide and take you to the Sacred Mountains where there is a great Medicine Lake where all the world is reflected."

When they arrived at Medicine Lake, the Wolf said to Jumping Mouse, "I must leave you now because I must return to guide others, but I will stay here with you as long as you wish."

"Thank you my Brother," said Jumping Mouse, trembling with fear. "Even though I am very frightened, I know you must return to show others the way to this place."

Jumping Mouse also knew it was no use running now because he was blind and he knew that an Eagle would find him. It wasn't long before he felt a shadow on his back and heard the swishing sound that Eagles make when they swoop down on their prey. As he braced himself for the blow, the Eagle hit and Jumping Mouse went to sleep. When he woke up, he was amazed to find that he was alive. Not only alive, but he could see again!

A blurry shape approached him and called out. "Hello Brother. Do you want some Medicine?" the Voice asked.

"Some Medicine for me? Oh, yes, thank you."

"Then crouch down as low as you can, then jump as high as you can," the Voice instructed him.

Jumping Mouse crouched as low as he could and then jumped. Suddenly, the wind caught him and carried him higher and higher.

"Do not be afraid," said the Voice. "Just hang onto the Wind and trust."

Jumping Mouse did as he was told and when he opened his eyes, everything was clear and the higher he went, the clearer everything became. When he looked below, he saw his old friend Frog sitting on a lily pad on the beautiful Medicine Lake.

"You now have a new name," Frog called out to him. "You are Eagle!"

WRITING EXERCISE: The Give Away

1. Many Native Americans have a tradition called "the Give-Away," which is a way of giving thanks for all that has been given them by sharing it or giving it away to others of their community. First write your takeaways from the story of Jumping Mouse who gave away both of his eyes to others. Think of an example from your own life in which you or someone you know demonstrated a great Give-Away and write about that.

2. The story of Little Mouse is a "teaching story." The narrator of this story tells his listeners that Mice only see clearly what is in front of then. Because of this limited way of seeing, they will always see and fear the spots in the sky, which in this case are the Eagles. Jumping Mouse, however, doesn't stay where everything is safe and in spite of his fear, runs out onto the open Prairie where he meets the Great Spirit's greatest gift to the people: the Buffalo, which represents the spirit of giving. The narrator explains that Mouse must give up one of his eyes, or his Mouse way of seeing in order to grow. One important lesson from the story, according to the narrator, is that people are never forced to do these things. Jumping Mouse, for example, could have remained hidden from Buffalo like Old Mouse chose to do. But to remain hidden can also have difficult consequences, such as seeing the Buffalo die and having to live with the stench of rotting flesh; or eventually experiencing thirst because the chokecherries would have made Jumping Mouse extremely thirsty for water.

How is the story of Jumping Mouse similar to a hero's journey in which a hero faces his worst fears in order to die to his old self and become a new, stronger person who is happy to give away or share his hard-won treasure with his community?

3. Think of a time in your life when you played it safe and what the consequences were as a result. Then, think of another time when you held your fear in check and took action anyway. How did you grow as a person as a result of thinking and acting past your fear?

4. Can you think of a time when you were blind to certain things in your life but once you let go of trying to control the situation and trusted, were able to fly like an Eagle?

ART EXERCISE: Making a Treasure Map

This easy and fun-to-make art exercise involves making a Treasure Map, sub-titled "What Do I Really Want?" A Treasure Map is a collection of images that serve as reflections of what we envision for ourselves in the future. Begin by collecting a number of magazines—the library sometimes has old issues it discards---and tear out any pictures that you are attracted to; then, add to this pile of pictures from the magazines any photos or fronts of old greeting cards you may have that appeal to you. Sort them all into categories, such as travel, home, career, health, friends, family, and so forth.

> Arrange the various images onto a large piece of construction paper, then cut and glue them to fit. You can write labels or captions under the images and enhance your Treasure Map in any other ways that appeal to you. Remember, this map is called "What Do I Really Want?" not "What Do I Think I Can Have?" Once you have completed your Treasure Map, hang it in a visible place where you can look at it often to affirm and remind yourself of the many "treasures" that await you.

> Some class participants have created a Treasure Chest or Box in which they place objects or images they like. Several people created a board game called Treasure Island, which they made by gluing their images onto a board, imagining themselves collecting various treasures as they went around the board.

 Answer the following questions about this exercise in your journal. How did you feel while selecting your images from the magazines? Did this exercise reveal any surprises about what you'd like for yourself now and in your future? Did you have any moments of feeling "I don't deserve this," or "This can't ever happen?" Write about these feelings of doubt or impossibility.

ART EXERCISE: Creating A "Found" Poem

Creating and writing a "found" poem is a lot of fun and can often provide profound insights regarding what we feel is important. It's also a way to integrate what you've learned in earlier phases of the writes of passage journey by creating a piece of writing that brings many of those ideas together in one poem. Begin by reviewing the readings, ideas, exercises and any notes you've made from the material we've covered so far in the workbook.

> Write out any phrases, words or ideas that had special meaning for you onto a piece of paper. Then, cut the words or phrases into strips. Spread all the small strips with the phrases or words written on them onto a larger piece of paper. Arrange and re-arrange them into a final form that appeals or makes sense to you. Finally, glue the strips onto the sheet of paper. Type up the words from the arrangement you've made from your strips of paper. You have now constructed a "found" poem, doing so in much the same way as a visual artist constructs a collage.

FOUND POEM

Inspired by Writes of Passage Course, October 2009
By Jo Bryant

You are creating your story
The intention is to trigger something
Opening you up to go a little deeper
It is time to speak the truth
Of your "soul loss" experience

We are born on this earth with no clear set of instructions
Maybe our desire is our only clue to navigate this
Labyrinth of life
Think of your plans as the dissected organs of a creature named Vision
Think of the lessons from the Wild Geese
And gifts from your imagination

What is the mythology of your ancestors?
What did you find out from doing the Life Map?
Make a Treasure Map for yourself
Create a life worth living on the long and winding roads

We are Volcanoes
We can choose. We can weave
Suffering comes into perspective
We can relax more deeply into our lives

If we don't tell the truth, who will?

You are the Divine Child
Spend some time alone every day
Live the questions now
Imagine what the world needs
What do you bring back to the community?

Work on Unfinished Business
Imagine your old age. What was your myth?
Write your epitaph. Keep it to one sentence
Remember the Village of precisely 100 people
Be good to each other

Gather yourselves!
Your playing small doesn't serve the world
Great love and great achievements involve great risks
Your consciousness is not just in your body. It is in everything
Mother Earth and Father Sky meet in our hearts and we know our wholeness.

Creating a Life Worth Living

Author and career consultant Carol Lloyd works to help people discover what career they have a passion for. Her book *Creating A Life Worth Living* presents helpful material for people to imagine possible futures for themselves. One exercise in particular that she uses to help people gain clarity about their career is called "three possible futures." Lloyd suggests that a person should choose three distinct sides of their personality, such as whimsical, practical and selfless. Although the three possible future career paths from three such different sides of ones personality might be similar in execution, they may be drastically different. For example, she says, you might use your skills as a graphic artist in all three possible futures mentioned above, only in different settings. The only requirement in the exercise is that each path must excite you enough to seriously consider it as a possibility for yourself.

I have adapted and used Lloyd's "three possible futures" exercises in the *Writes of Passage* classes many times and people have found them to be enormously valuable. One of the positive aspects of the "three possible futures" exercise is that it allows for letting your instinctual desires for certain dreams to arise and find their voice or expression without the judgments or labels we often put on them, such as being too unrealistic or selfish.

WRITING EXERCISE: Three Possible Futures

Begin by sitting quietly for some moments, letting your body and mind relax. In the space below or in your journal, write on the top of three separate pages, *Path One*, *Path Two*, and *Path Three*. Leave several blank pages in between each section to fully explore the three paths. Decide what you want to call each possible future path, such as Graphics Artist, Game Creator, and Art Teacher. Place the name of each career path at the top of each of the three sections. Write about each path with a non-judgmental mind when answering the following questions.

PATH ONE: Think back to your childhood when a teacher or other adult asked you what you wanted to be when you grew up. What was your answer?

____

____

____

____

____

____

____

____

____

____

____

PATH TWO: Ask yourself what you would like to accomplish on this life path in one year? In five years? In ten years?

PATH THREE: List any advantages and disadvantages to this life plan. How do you feel writing about this plan right now? If the plan doesn't net you a livable income right away, how would you earn a living during this process? What holds you back from doing your dream? What are you afraid of? What do you really feel inspired to do? What is your "acorn" destiny? Does this job nurture your soul?

Here is one class participant's writing in which she explores possible futures for herself as she ages:

Exploring Possible Features

This assignment was troublesome for me. I think it has something to do with my age. Having just turned 70 this week has influenced my feelings about the details of the assignment. "Planning into the future 10 years ahead…" feels daunting right now. The futures that I would want to invest energy in are more in the world of fantasy than possibility.

The other hesitation is that I have been goal setting with great intent, pushing to completion, creating, problem solving and making things happen most of my adult life. Sometimes, using plain old elbow grease to make it all work.

A few years ago, I decided to try a different way, because I realized that my efforts had been colored by the word SHOULD. I should have a passion, a plan, a pursuit. That unconscious mandate began to wear and tear on my spirit and physical body, not to mention the SHOULD of…"what will others think of me if I am not ambitious, working hard or, passionate?"

I have never been personally ambitious. I think of myself as a visionary. When an idea would arrive that seemed workable I'd give it a shot. I would not spend much time arguing for its pragmatism. Mostly, I have been inspired and when the inspiration arrived, I was pretty fearless. I have always been curious, committed and willing to work hard and enthusiastically at any idea that ignited my creative interest. Somehow I have been successful at most of what I have devoted my life to.

Living and surviving put so many boundaries in place to stay on track with what was working, so, I tried to avoid being distracted by what came drifting by.

Now, I am moving from a different center. My desire is to be SPIRIT DRIVEN, to be open to what comes, then to pause and reflect on the FEEL of it. Earlier in life, the idea would arrive and I would immediately get to work to make it come to fruition. I needed what I created to be able to support me financially. I have luxury now to allow and follow, rather than react and pursue.

So, the idea of exploring possible futures seems counter productive to my current philosophy. I would like to give myself the freedom to follow whatever feels larger than I can imagine.

However, I can list some things, that if they came floating by, I would be attracted to them.

I would love to move somewhere that has an abundance of water, a lush, moist environment, near either a lake or an ocean. I would like to live in a town, a small city or community, where I would be able to walk to nearby places, or ride a city bus as my means of getting around. I would love to take advantage of the social and cultural activity such a place would offer. I would want to live in a smaller house that has a smaller environmental footprint. I want a garden with vegetables, herbs and flowers. I would be open to sharing this space with others as a more economical use of resources. In fact, if this could be in a community of like minded others with similar intentions, that would be ideal.

I would continue to create, draw, and craft whatever interests me, and find possibilities to market my creations.

Living in this place I would have access to becoming a NIA teacher and would teach NIA to older people in a variety of venues, earning some income.

My husband would have a personality transplant and he would be in love with helping orchestrate and participate in this new life.

I would love to be a grandmother and live close to my grandchild so that I could help out and simply enjoy being active in my grandchild's life. And if that would happen, this fantasy would become my number one priority.

Currently, the possible future that is underway is the completion of the deck of cards I have been working on for 20 years. My hope is that they become a teaching tool for women and that I will create numerous workshops and discussion groups for years to come. I will sell the decks and charge for the workshops and travel to teach and present. My Social Security pension can more than keep me financially viable as my decks sell and workshops fill.

It is unsettling for me to apply a timeline to any of these imaginings other than the cards.

I will be meeting with the graphic artist in August who will finalize the layout for the book and cards. My goal is to have the deck ready by spring of 2019.

[NOTE: Elizabeth's Deck of Cards did become a reality! You can order them at DreamingAtTheWell.com]

ALTERNATIVE... EXPLORING

I realized that the futures I have been considering were all colored by the presence of my husband in my life. So, I am giving myself permission to create futures that are not hemmed in by being married to him, as if I were a single woman in the world right now.

First: I would explore all the ways to travel that would take me to different countries or places within the US. There are dozens of programs that I could participate in that provide free room and board for helping out in some fashion at the destination. I would love to do that for a year. I would sublet where I was living or even participate in a vacation rental home exchange.

Second: I would move to a much smaller house closer to my daughter in Albuquerque. I would create a garden that would feed me for most of the year. I would get involved in community projects, go to some continuing education classes, join dance classes, take advantage of the opportunities offered by the senior centers. I would have my friends over for dinner. I would simply enjoy being involved with life.

Third: I would consider joining SENIOR AMERICORE.

I would not have a pet and if my daughter would have a baby all plans to travel would be canceled for a while.

Elizabeth Prospaio
March 2018

Using Archetypes as A Guide to Your Life's Work

Laurence Boldt, author of *Zen and the Art of Making a Living: A Practical Guide to Creative Career Design* encourages us to think of our lives as a great work of art and to recognize how universal energies play out in the particulars of our own life. He uses the three elements of myth, archetype and symbol as a framework to consider four universal or archetypal energies that an individual can use to create their life's work. Those four archetypes named and described by Boldt are: the **Hero**, who is the decision-maker and seeker of the Grail, symbol of knowledge and a willingness to undertake the journey into the world of the unknown; the **Magician/Shaman** who uses the creative power of imagination and magic to bring about the changes she wishes to unfold in her life; the **Warrior** who uses the creative power of purposeful action to achieve his purpose; and, the **Scholar** who uses her creative power of learning and teaching as a tool for self-transformation to find her life's soul work. According to Boldt, the **Hero** decides the direction and what to create; the **Magician** develops the magic to use; the **Warrior** carries out the plan; and the **Scholar** keeps everything on track. Using these four archetypal models, Boldt says, is a way to put into a practical context the inquiry into your life's purpose that can lead to putting soul into your work.

WRITING EXERCISE: Four Archetypes

Using the information above, write about the four archetypes of Hero/Heroine, Magician/Shaman, Warrior, and Scholar in your journal or the spaces below. Describe how each archetype is present in your life and, letting your imagination guide you, write what you see each one creating and accomplishing in your life. You may decide to write the archetypes into a myth with you as the main character. If so, remember to use any symbols that come to you. Glue or draw any images that represent any of the archetypes.

HERO/HEROINE

____

____

____

____

93

WARRIOR

SCHOLAR

Here is one class participant's writing in which she explores possible futures for herself as she ages:

USING ARCHETYPES AS A GUIDE TO YOUR LIFE'S WORK

I have used the archetype of HEROINE most of my life to bring me to where I am today. I was the brave sister protector as a child to my siblings. I was a HEROINE in every sport I played. I never gave up and was a master at knowing all the strategies of the game. I knew the workings of every position and was the leader on the field. I never lacked confidence or doubted myself in the game.

The HEROINE in me was the wanderlust I felt as I ventured off to college and away from home for the first time. College was the last place I wanted to go, I hated schoolwork with a passion and was never fully committed to it. What I really wanted was to drive off into the sunset towards California with my best friend and partner in crime, Sandy. But given the fact that my dad was of Irish immigrants, not going to college was not an option. So off I went wrapped in my WARRIOR cloak to New Hampshire to attend Franklin Pierce College, which began 2 ½ years of discovery and not much schoolwork. It was a small school of under a thousand students in the middle of nowhere and had no athletics except intermural sports. Sports was what I did and how I identified myself so I put on my WARRIOR cloak and mustered up all the aggressive energy I needed to compete in a Boy's world; something I was very versed in from having grown up battling with boys my whole life. (I want to take a minute to thank all those boys that helped me become the warrior princess I am to this day.)

Growing up, teenage boys who lived in the nearby neighborhood, much to my mom's horror came to pick me up and walk me to the tackle football games we engaged in for the five years I lived there. I was 9 years old at the beginning and a fierce competitor. These boys put up with the laughs and ridicule about having a GIRL on their team, because once the game began and I rocked the other team with touchdown passes caught, thrown and tackles I made, they never laughed again. They all were really nice to me and when the game was over, they walked me back home, much to my mother's delight, but not really! She never knew how to handle that WARRIOR princess heroine-returned-from-battle child who so delighted in that role.

That WARRIOR and triumphant HEROINE were honed on the battlefields of sports. Since the moment I discovered that I could run, jump and play ball better than all the girls and just as good as most boys, I grabbed hold of those skills and ran and ran through, towards, and away from my life. I fought tooth and nail to enter every game. The MAGICIAN in me always found a way to participate against the stacked odds of "No girls allowed; we don't want to play with a girl; she's gonna cry; she'll be no good" and on and on." Yawn.

But I came up with a plan to overcome these objections. First, I would find the game anywhere I was: any school, any yard, any state in the country. I'd sit off in the distance observing and waiting to make my move. Once I had the plan mapped out, I'd move in for the execution. Now these boys just thought I was some girl watching them play so they'd get all full of themselves and that's when the mistake would happen. The ball would get past them so I would pick it up and throw the football, perfect spiral 20-30 yards back to them. Mouths dropped, then they'd take a moment to look at each other and finally say, "Wow! Great arm. You wanna play?"

It never failed. I pegged a throw to the cut-off boy with the baseball, drain a three point shot from out of bounds, kick a bend-it-like-beckam soccer pass, you name it. I could nail it.

This was also how I got on the Kobabas brothers all men's flag football team in college. Being the only girl was quite a crowd gatherer. It was also true when on Martha's Vineyard, I played in the all-men's fast pitch softball league and once again became the talk of the island.

One of the most amazing pieces of magic was how Rugby came into my life. I was living in Madison, Wisconsin and my partner at the time was in a dance therapy program at the University. The dance department was located in the same building with the athletic department. One day she came home with a flyer. "I think you should check this out. You might love this sport."

Although I knew nothing about rugby, it turned out to be a match made in heaven. Being a sports junkie, I jumped into the next practice, which became my passion for the next 13 years and brought my lust for adventure to the forefront of my life. I worked to travel from state to state with each of my teams. The sense of family with the rugby community was what I had searched for through all my years in sports; the sense of belonging that came from being the athlete that I was, helped me channel the fighting WARRIOR into the focused WARRIOR, lessons that would help propel me towards the doctor that I would eventually become.

I had no idea what was ahead but the strength that I gained from fitting into something without a fight was life altering. I call rugby "organized anarchy" and it fit into my sense of freedom and justice like a glove. The other thing that was so amazing was that for the first time I was able to play on the pitch, that's what the rugby field is called, with 14 other women athletes. I was able to play tackle football with women, which was a life-altering revelation for me. The thing that set me apart from a lot of others was that I was a great tackler, maybe because of the hundreds of hours spent watching football with my dad, both live and on TV. It's a connection that lives on today with my sisters.

The last archetype of SCHOLAR is the one I struggle with most. It was the word itself that I had to get over in order to write about it. I wrote every other archetype first and kept coming back to the SCHOLAR. In my family, we had no scholars that had to do with intelligence. I never liked school because of the rules and the cramping of my style. I realize that the SCHOLAR as archetype is the path that the universe had mapped out for me, however, that I wasn't aware of. But as I look back on this master plan, the SCHOLAR in me had all the smarts I needed to stay on track.

When I was accepted to acupuncture school after 2 ½ years at one college, then going back to school 10 years later to finish the degree, I knew it still wasn't right. I wasn't any closer to figuring out what I wanted to be when I grew up. Then the SCHOLAR revealed the plan and I found my calling at the Southwest Acupuncture College in Santa Fe, NM. The magic had happened and I listened.

Acupuncture school was so foreign literally and figuratively, yet somehow I just knew it was what I had prepared my whole life for. It was instinctual and easy for me in so many ways. The learning was from somewhere deep inside me. It was intuitive and I was good at it. It was really the first time I felt this way about school. The SCHOLAR had been there all along making sure I stayed on track even though so much of what I heard about was how I was doing my life all-wrong. My dad always used to say to me, "When are you going to grow up and get a real job?"

About three years ago, my brother, two sisters and I were sitting together having our tea and coffee when my younger sister reflected on how proud mom and dad would be of us all. We like each other and we are all kind, funny, giving human beings, which is a direct result of my parents being good and caring people. As I was taking in her comments, I thought about the Doctor I am today and said something to the effect about my dad's words about "growing up and getting a real job."

"Oh, poor dad," my brother Gary said. "He didn't realize he could only ask for one of those things."

We all had a double over laugh on that one. It was in that moment that I realized how far I had come and how we just have to keep following The Magic.

Dairne McLoughlin
March 2018

My True Work

Michel and Justine Toms are co-founders of New Dimensions Radio in San Francisco. In their book called *True Work* they define what the soul of work actually is. In a chapter titled, "Sacred Labor, the Soul of Work," they speak about the need to recognize our inherent connections to the invisible realm or spiritual world that can greatly enhance our creative intelligence. They emphasize that regular attention to prayer, meditation, reflection, dreams, sacred rituals, offerings and solitude are ways to keep that connection to the invisible world and to honor its energies. While never specifically defining spirituality, they instead give numerous examples of how to connect to the invisible realms in order to live an authentic life.

WRITING EXERCISE: Four Archetypes

Using the idea of "Sacred Labor, the Soul of Work," write about a way that you have or would like to begin to honor the soul of your work and the work of your soul. Begin by identifying what the term "soul of work" means to you.

____

____

____

____

____

____

____

Here are two examples written in response to the writing exercise *The Work of My Soul.*

The Work of My Soul

The gift of tuning into the rhythms and textures of life brings a gratitude for small things that bring great joy. When we clear our minds of what we think we ought to be consumed with, it leaves an open slate for direct experience where we can be washed by pure sensation. I close my eyes and focus on beauty and the swirl of life unfolding and the words just tumble.

Nutmeg in coffee
Dew clinging to grass
Eucalyptus fog
Toes making imprints in saturated sand at waves' edge
The moment of ahhh in the body immersing in hot bath
A cheek-to-cheek hug
Eye locking gazes in the span of two heartbeats
Fresh cherries leaving their dye on fingers and lips

The light at dusk like stage lighting
The rhythm of train sound clacking on tracks passing by, its feel in my body
Self-soothing vocalizations that come on their own
Wind that makes leaves dance in a swirl
Moments when two people look at each other without knowing why and share an understanding
450 nanometers of light: the special green hue of new growth in spring

Dance that expresses not only my own heart but the heart of the people, now and way back through time
The aroma of spices cooking in the pot
The pull of the waves at shore around my ankles
Racing down to the beach with my kids
Freshly cut evergreen boughs
The breath pattern that sends peace to my cells

Soft rose petals that draw my fingers to the bud
Dripping springs on lush green moss
Sandstone dust as rock disintegrates and goes aloft on wind
Harmony of voices building strength as the power it brings to singers expands
The thrill of the gift, given and received
Pure maple syrup in coffee

Blueberries freshly raked in Maine with scent of the yonder coast
Spinning to find the very center of calm

The aroma of freshly baked pie
Staring into the fire and finding ancestors
The grace in walking fine lines
Touching a newborn's head as it emerges
The well of the Om as changed
Watching the back of my hand over the years as I age
The crisp edge of dawn, a vehicle for prayers
Finding a wild bird feather at my feet
Trust falling with a solid friend
The echoes of my flute reverberating in layered canyon walls
The steady pulse of the Earth.

Rebecca Leeman
April 2018

Here is the second example:

The Work of My Soul

I have never been able to do soulless work of any kind for very long. If I did work, JUST A JOB, I would watch the death march of enthusiasm, hope, and fulfillment heading for the horizon. Then my soul would sit me down and in a wave of sadness and misery, let me know I was leaving it behind.

I have been molded by my very pushy soul for most of my adult life, even when it appeared to my ego that I was impractical and possibly very unstable and why didn't I want to sell myself so I could have the stuff everyone else had?

It is curious as I review my life, that I have always been able to make a living creatively since I was in my twenties. Jobs were in support of my artistic ideas and I never felt interested in having a career. I was more comfortable figuring life out for myself.

I have been content living economically small, but creatively large. I have been blessed by forces greater than myself that have miraculously kept me afloat and a creative soul that would settle for nothing less than strict adherence to its mandate.

However, in the world of loving and being loved, nothing happened according to my plans. My soul had another idea entirely. It seems my soul growth love plan was to learn from betrayal, disappointment and heart-break, in a way I could never have imagined. The push has been to become my own best parent, lover and companion. And that journey continues.

AND NOW WHAT?

My work is to gather all I have learned, one piece at a time, into a Bundle named MY LIFE and to allow myself to be shown where to deposit my wisdom.

Somehow, all of this soul growth has worked itself into an intricate weaving that has become animated by living. It is no longer imperative to try to understand how or why, but to follow the thread as it weaves me deeper and deeper into the body of my earth mother.

Elizabeth Prosapio
April 2018

PHASE FIVE
Putting Your Wisdom to Work:
Making an Act of Power

We are volcanoes.
When we offer our experience as our truth,
all the maps change.
There are new mountains.
That's what I want---To hear you erupting.
You Mount St. Helenses who don't know
the power in you---I want to hear you.
If we don't tell our truth, who will?
... Ursula K. LeGuin

I will act as if what I do makes a difference.
...William James

What is an act of power? An act of power is anything we accomplish that demands our courage and commitment; anything that requires an enormous effort to complete and a willingness to be noticed by offering and sharing our creation out into the world. I first read about making an act of power in the book *Teachings Around the Sacred Wheel* by author and medicine woman Lynn Andrews. Andrews says that finding your act of power in the world gives you a point of view, a starting place where you can begin to get comfortable with success in your life. This is important whether you want to become a chef, homemaker, actress, or politician, she says. An act of power requires extraordinary focus and demands all your will to accomplish it. To be secure in your physical life, you have to know your destiny or life's purpose, a topic we explored in some detail in *Finding the Soul of Your Work*. An act of power goes one step further by providing a mirror to learn more about yourself because, by creating an act of power through your own effort and focus, you are requiring yourself to take a stand and be noticed for your power. For many people, especially women who have often been encouraged to play a background role, being noticed and affirmed publically is difficult to do.

Getty Images
Public Domain

How One Queen's Act of Power Changed Ancient Hawaii

Maxine Mrantz's book *Women of Old Hawaii* tells the stories of many of the outstanding women of old Hawaii including the last monarch, Queen Liliuokalani, deposed in 1898 and a republic was declared.

Wikimedia commons
Public Domain/Lithograph of Queen Kaahumanu
by Jean de la Gourdaine

Mrantz gives many insights into what life was like for women of those early times, both those of royal blood as well as the commoners. The idea female beauty for the ancient Hawaiians, for example, was a woman of great height, at least 6-feet tall and of generous proportions. The heavier the woman was, especially the chiefesses, the closer to the gods she was considered to be. Women pursued active lifestyles such as swimming, surfing, climbing, fishing and engaged in the other games played in the islands. Women also worked at the difficult tasks of kapa-beating, root mashing, and mat plaiting as well as engaging in the arts of hula dancing and chanting.

Before the missionaries came to Hawaii and the women adopted their style of wearing apparel, Hawaiian women wore the pa'u, a wrap-around garment several layers thick made from kapa cloth. The highborn women wore wreaths of feathers or flowers on their heads and were bare breasted except for flower leis worn around their neck. A chiefess might also wear a neckpiece made of numerous strands of braided human hair fastened by a pendant carved from the tooth of a whale to indicate her high rank. The common women were scantily dressed or naked.

Descent came through the female and sacred bloodlines were of great importance. A mate of a chief or chiefess couldn't be of too low in rank or it was considered a disgrace and any child born from such a union would be unfit to rule and would be put to death. In order to preserve the bloodline, members of the same family often married a sibling. Although plural marriages did exist, mostly only the royal families or chiefs and wealthy people practiced it.

Because women were considered to be less pleasing to the gods, they had a lower status than men and weren't allowed to eat with them. They also weren't allowed to eat certain foods, such as bananas. Even the royal women known as *alii* were under this same *kapu*. Disobedience of these laws or *kapus* could result in death.

But there was one woman who changed all that, which brings us to our story of Queen Kaahumanu.

Queen Kaahumanu of Ancient Hawaii
(Adapted from Maxine Mrantz's book *Women of Old Hawaii*)

Queen Kaahumanu was the favorite wife of the king of Old Hawaii, Kamehameha I, and was the first official woman lawmaker in the land. Standing over 6 ft. tall and weighing over 300 pounds, she was revered not only for her beauty but also for her intelligence and fearlessness. After the king's death, she dressed herself in his magnificent warrior feathered cape, took his spear and placed his warrior helmet on her head. These were all audacious acts for anyone, reminding us of another female heroine, Joan of Arc of France. Kaahumanu, dressed like a man, went directly to the young king Liholiho and told him that it was his father's last wish that they should both rule the kingdom together. The young king and all the royal alii accepted her proclamation of rulership and she became the Kuhina-Nui, second in command.

But this fearless act of power was only the beginning of the many changes Queen Kaahumanu brought to women and the Hawaiian culture. The first major change began when she broke the eating kapu. Both Kaahumanu and Liholiho's mother Queen Keopuolani suffered feelings of shame and humiliation at the eating kapu forbidding certain foods to women such as bananas. One day Kaahumanu ate a banana in front of King Liholiho, which he ignored. Later his own mother sat and ate with his younger brother and again the King did nothing. The two strong women slowly wore the young king down and later at a banquet, Liholiho went to the women's table, sat down and ate with them. Although the people were astounded, they soon followed suit and men and women began to eat together.

Kaahumanu demonstrated the growing amount of political power she had achieved by not only overthrowing the eating kapu but eventually the entire kapu system. Soon the restrictions for their old religious customs and beliefs were thrown out as well. With Kaahumanu's approval, the high priests toppled the many stone images of their gods placed in their heiaus and threw them into the ocean. It wasn't long however, before the missionaries arrived and began to replace this religious vacuum with Protestant Christianity, establishing themselves and their beliefs in the islands. They opened schools for the children where they were taught to read and write and soon naked women and children began wearing bonnets and muu-muus or long dresses and started going to church.

Kaahumanu's relationship with the Protestant Christians was tentative at first. Stories tell of her making a social call to the Missionary's hone after surfing, arriving completely naked! She also didn't renounce all the old ways of her people and culture. She decided she wanted to marry the King of Kauai and after enticing him aboard her ship, sailed back to Honolulu with him on board. Then, in what may have been an astute political move, she decided she would also marry his handsome son and brought him back to Honolulu and married him as well, leaving Kauai with no leader to rule the island. She showed off her two husbands by arriving at church riding in the first carriage ever brought to Hawaii. Soon one of her own staff was installed as ruler of Kauai, giving her rulership of two of Hawaii's islands.

In the years that followed the ending of kapus and abandonment of the old religions, and with the influx of trading vessels and whaling ships in the harbors, the quality of life had deteriorated and spiraled downwards into lawlessness, drunkenness and violence. Hawaiian men now did menial jobs for the traders and ship captains and women went out to the ships and slept with the whalers, often contracting and spreading venereal disease. Kaahumanu realized she had to do something; that there needed to be a code of law to restore order.

She decided to base that law on the missionaries' Ten Commandments from their Bible. Appointing her brother to oversee the enforcement of the new law code, order slowly began to be restored.

As she aged Kaahumanu became more devoted to the religion of the missionaries and primarily due to her influence, Hawaii became a Protestant state. Schools and churches started by missionaries were supported and maintained by the alii. She believed that Hawaii's future lay with the lifestyle and beliefs of the missionaries. Because she was fearless and smart, she instigated changes to Hawaii's culture that forever changed the way people lived and how women were treated. When she died in 1832, she had influenced and changed Hawaiian life more than any other ruler or woman ever had, or as some might say, ever has.

WRITING EXERCISES: Acts of Power

Queen Kaahumanu demonstrated many Acts of Power, beginning with her declaration that she should share rulership with the dead king's son.

> Write about one of the Acts of Power achieved by Queen Kaahumanu that seems the most extraordinary to you. Why did you choose that specific act? Is there anything you've done in your life that took great courage on your part to achieve? What enabled you to make such an act?

> Do you think people who demonstrate in public protests against social injustice and racism are committing Acts of Power? Have you ever participated in a public protest of any kind? Under what circumstances would you consider such an act?

TWO PART VISUALIZATION EXERCISE: Your Act of Power

Read through this visualization first and decide if you can remember the main segments before
continuing with the exercise. Or, you may want to record the visualization into a tape recorder and play
it back. Another possibility is to share this exercise with someone else as you take turns experiencing
the visualization and talking about it afterwards.

PART ONE

> Close your eyes and begin by taking a few deep breaths and letting yourself relax. Visualize what
> your act of power in the world might be. Relax and simply let the ideas and images come to you
> without grasping or trying to hold onto any of them. Watch them float by as you might watch slow
> frames in a movie. As you relax further into the visualization, recall a time in your life when you
> were most excited about something you were doing, or when you were a part of something a group
> was doing that was exciting to you.

> When this image is clear, open your eyes and write in your journal/workbook what you saw. What
> was the situation and what were you doing? Who was there with you? How did you feel when you
> remembered this event?

> Continue with your visualization by closing your eyes again and letting yourself drift into a quiet reverie, relaxing your mind without trying to control your thoughts. Think back to a time or situation in which you felt powerful. Let those feelings of powerfulness surround you. Feel them seeping into your skin as well as your mind and heart. Repeat to yourself: *I am powerful, I am powerful.* Notice any thoughts that come up to dispute that statement. Watch them come and go as you continue to repeat the mantra *I am powerful.* When you have completely identified with and absorbed the feelings of personal power inside yourself, slowly open your eyes, take a moment to reorient yourself, then write what you experienced as you repeated the mantra *I am powerful.* Did you have any more insights into what your act of power is or what is holding you back from expressing your act of power out into the world?

____

____

____

____

____

____

____

____

____

____

____

____

____

Who Can Be Powerful?

Sometimes people are under the false impression that in order for them to be powerful, someone else has to be less powerful in some way. It's an old thought form that no longer serves us. Books such as Riane Eisler's *The Chalice and the Blade,* Starhawk's *Dreaming the Dark* and the *Course In Miracles* have pointed out the fallacy of this outworn notion that only some people can have power. Eisler tells us that in goddess-worshipping cultures during ancient times, there existed a model of society that was grounded in partnership wherein social relations were based primarily on the principle of linking rather than ranking. She called this way of relating a *partnership model,* which she said is in direct contrast to the currently popular *dominator model* where ranking is constantly being made of one half of humanity over the other.

Starhawk, a popular witch, author and political activist who lives in the Bay area, has also spoken about the idea of having "power with" rather than "power over" as a model of how we can interact with one another. She explains that one person standing tall in her power doesn't mean that someone else has to be diminished in any way.

The popular book called *A Course In Miracles* also states a similar principle: standing tall in your power doesn't diminish anyone, but rather gives everyone permission to do the same. We saw those same sentiments being expressed in Nelson Mandala's acceptance speech quoted earlier in the workbook. Everyone can be powerful.

WRITING & VISUALIZATION EXERCISE: Making An Act of Power

You have thought about and visualized what your act of power is. With this exercise you will take it a step further by imagining how you will send it forth into the world to be noticed by numerous others. Although there are many ways to be noticed out in the world, being on the cover of a major magazine for example, denotes some noteworthy accomplishment.

> Close your eyes and take a few deep breaths. Imagine yourself on the cover of a major magazine that you read or respect. See the photo of yourself in as much vivid detail as possible: What are you wearing? Where was the picture taken? What would the caption and description underneath your picture read? Open your eyes and write your answers to the questions above.

> Write several paragraphs that describe in more detail what your act of power is that resulted in your being featured on the cover of a favorite magazine.

Making Your Act of Power: A Beautiful Example

One former writer in the *Writes of Passage* class called her Act of Power *The Magnificent Appreciation Project*. She saw herself featured on the cover of "O" Magazine with the caption and words underneath her photo reading, "Local Heroine Receives Award: This is the story of an ordinary woman making an extraordinary impact on the world. In March of 2009, Shirley Chavez of Albuquerque declared that she wanted to make an Act of Power in the world that has achieved amazing results in the state of New Mexico and is rapidly spreading to people worldwide. It all began when she decided to test her Appreciation Theory."

Shirley went on to write her imagined interview inside 'O' magazine that detailed her *Magnificent Appreciation Project* and the results. Because it is so inspiring, I've included the "interview" here.

Magnificent Appreciation Project's Shirley Chavez
Interview with 'O' Magazine

'O' Magazine: *What did you set out to do back in March of 2009?*

Shirley: *I thought that by testing a particular theory, I could make a difference in the world.*

'O' Magazine: *What was the theory?*

Shirley: *I call it "The Appreciation Theory."*

'O' Magazine: *What is "The Appreciation Theory?"*

Shirley: *The theory says that the word "appreciation" carries the highest vibration of any word in the English language. And that acts of appreciation carry the highest vibration of any other act.*

'O' Magazine: *How did you test your theory?*

Shirley: *I started out by listing 10 things I would do to stand in my power and foster the expression of appreciation in my own life.*

'O' Magazine: *What were some of the things on your list?*

Shirley: *Here is my list of ten things:*
       1. I "eat, drink, and sleep" appreciation! Just like salespeople do. They "eat, drink and sleep" sales.

2.	*I fully appreciate the magnificence of "what is"---of what I already have in my life.*

3.	*Every day, I write down 10 things I appreciate.*

4.	*Express appreciation every time I pay a bill or spend money on anything.*

5.	*Express appreciation every time I receive money, whether it is my salary or money from another source.*

6.	*Strike up conversations with perfect strangers about appreciation.*

7.	*Write in my journal regularly about appreciation. Document times when I expressed and received appreciation.*

8.	*Share my vision about the project with others.*

9.	*Give progress report every week and get feedback from my business support group.*

10.	*Revise my plan as new information comes to light.*

'O' Magazine:	*What was the result of doing those things?*

Shirley:	*Twelve months ago, I couldn't have conceived how magnificent the results would be! As it turned out, the more appreciation I expressed, the more I received back. The flow of appreciation came back to me in many forms. Every time I expressed appreciation, my capacity to express and receive appreciation actually expanded. When I dramatically increased my expression of appreciation, the flow of appreciation that came back to me dramatically increased. This appreciation game has become an amazing accomplishment, a brilliant creation that leaves me in absolute awe of every moment. Tremendous appreciation has been reflected back to me from other people. It is happening in the form of compliments, kindness, special favors, love, and gratitude. Even in the form of money!*

'O' MAGAZINE:	*This sounds amazing!*

SHIRLEY:	*I only did the 10 things I mentioned to you. And what happened was that the more I talked with people, the more the idea caught on fire. People literally got inspired. What has happened in 12 short months is that other people have taken on this whole idea of expressing appreciation. We eventually formed a non-profit corporation. We* *have lots of people on our team who have great ideas about expressing appreciation, thereby transforming relationships and the energy on the planet!*

*If you were to come to Albuquerque, you would see billboards all over the city advertising **Magnificent Appreciation Project**. That name was coined by one of my friends and has been embraced by schools, churches, government offices, private businesses, and many individuals. All of these entities have reported extreme improvement of morale and production in all departments. The ranks of the **Magnificent Appreciation Project** have grown by leaps and bounds. There are hundreds of people involved, and the plan is to expand into all cities in New Mexico. After that, we expect to take it all over the United States and   then into Canada, Mexico and other countries. The effects of this project have been astounding. We never dreamed it would grow so quickly and make a difference in so many lives.*

Shirley identified specific things that she had to give up or let go in order to perform her act of power. Here they are:

1. *Shyness*
2. *Old beliefs about myself that don't serve me*
3. *Belief that I have no power, creativity and ingenuity*
4. *Perceived limitations*
5. *Desire and tendency to hide my power and awareness of who I really am*
6. *Being unforgiving towards myself and others*
7. *Fear of my own power*

ART ACTIVITY: Creating An Empowerment Ceremony

Once you are clear what your act of power in the world is to be, you can create a ritual or ceremony of empowerment to help ground your ideas. For this ritual ceremony of empowerment, you will create two lists on small pieces of paper. On the first list, write down 10 specific things you are going to do by this time next year to make your act of power happen. On the second list, write out the things you're going to give away or release that have kept you from making your act of power---things like "I'm not good enough;" "People will criticize me;" "I'm afraid of being successful;" or, "I don't like to be noticed."

An Artist's Workspace: Photo by Marjorie St. Clair

Find and decorate two objects such as an ordinary stick, rock or small box. Wrap, tie or glue your lists onto the two objects. Once you have your two lists attached to your decorated objects, take them to a special place in your home, garden or out into nature where you won't be disturbed. In order to create or mark off the setting for your ceremony as a special or sacred place, you will set the circle energetically by placing stones, feathers or rocks in a circle large enough for you to sit inside it. Once you've done this, sit down inside the circle and then sing, pray, read a poem or simply sit quietly. This is your ceremony of empowerment and is self-generated as you are guided in the moment. Do what feels natural and comfortable to you. The intention here is to empower yourself and to acknowledge how serious you are about making your act of power in the world. Simple is good!

> First, you want to release any old or negative thoughts and ideas that have held you back. Read out loud the ten items on your list that you want to release and acknowledge any feelings that might come up such as sadness, anger, regret or grief. In order to leave behind all that has hindered you in the past from accomplishing your act of power, you can bury the list in the ground, burn it up or tear it into pieces to burn later when you're in a safe place for burning.

> Take the second object that you've attached the list of things you will accomplish for your act of power within a year's time. Read the list out loud. Again, notice how you feel---scared, critical, overwhelmed, joyful, relieved or excited?

> When you feel complete with the ceremony, make a mental note of everything that has happened. If you were outside, what birds or animals showed up? What about the weather, wind, or clouds? If you were inside, did you forget to turn off your cell phone? Did someone unexpectedly knock on your door? Did you notice a heightened sense of energy enter your space?

> To close the ceremony, express your gratitude in some way. For example, if you did the ceremony outside, bless the circle before you de-construct it. Then, record everything that happened by answering the questions above in your journal or workbook. Embellish with artwork, drawings or paste pictures that symbolize your experience.

PHASE SIX

Becoming An Elder—Loving Yourself and Serving Others

Jane Goodall,
By U.S. Department of State
Public domain

I don't know what your destiny will be, but one thing I do know;
the only ones among you who will be really happy are those
who sought and found how to serve.
...Albert Schweitzer

Taking Inventory for Act Three

As we saw earlier, an important challenge of mid-life was to discover a new dream for life's second half, but what about the challenge for life when one becomes an elder and is in Act Three of their life? What are the dreams and realities of life supposed to look like then in the last cycle of life? This is a good time to take out the Life Map you made earlier and review your life's pathway up to this point. Just as the generations now in mid-life are shattering the old stereotypes of aging, so too are the aging "baby boomers" shattering what the last cycle of life can look like.

WRITING EXERCISE: Taking Inventory

In your journal or in the workbook, answer the following questions:

1. What will I be doing when I'm no longer spending most of my time at the work I'm doing now? What's left for me to do that I haven't done that I'd still like to do? What's on my bucket list?

2. If you're already retired, how have the days been passing? Does what you anticipated for this time in your life match the reality you're experiencing?

3. Even if you don't consider yourself to be a wise elder, what do you want to leave behind as your heritage or gift to others?

4. How important is it to you to focus on the spiritual aspect of your life at this time?

Looking Forward: Age Is An Attitude

It's important to understand how our beliefs and feelings about aging shape the way we create our lives as we age. Poet and author May Sarton once said, "I suppose old age begins when one looks backward rather than forward, but I look forward with joy to the years ahead and especially to the surprises that any day may bring." People born in the post-WWII baby boom years of the late 1940s, became a driving force in the sixties and are still going strong in the early part of the twenty-first century! With advances in science, medicine and preventive health care, the boomer's generation was the first to have high expectations of growing older and many, like May Sarton, are models for living well into old age by looking forward instead of to the past.

Despite all the evidence and intellectual energy and activism apparent in the boomers, however, the specter of aging remains colored by the historic assumption that aging is defined by difficulty and is something to be dreaded. Most people until recently dreaded aging because they saw it as a decline into disease and disability. One need only look at our commercials, movies, and magazines that almost exclusively deify youth as the only desirable age to be, while denying or putting down the reality of aging. Women more often than men have suffered from this anti-aging attitude and the desire to stay young no matter the cost. Wrinkles, often seen on men as an honored badge of having lived an extraordinary, exciting life, are considered something women should hide with make-up or plastic surgery. Although cosmetic plastic surgery has never been more popular with people of all ages and genders, millions of women "of a certain age" look to cosmetic surgery to restore them to their former youthful beauty.

That advancing in age could offer exciting opportunities for personal growth and profound satisfaction seems a foreign idea to many. Even as we are made aware almost everyday of new scientific and medical advances that can prolong life, we also know that living longer can be a burden or a blessing, depending on how we regard it. As we face into the truth of becoming an elder, we are especially interested in the quality of our lives, rather than just how many more days or years we might be able to live. In this last phase of our lives, our worth in life depends largely on how productive we continue to be and how loved and loving we feel. Feelings of self-worth and excitement about the future far transcend high cholesterol, heart rate, bone density and sagging body parts.

History offers remarkable stories that illustrate the potential for intellectual and emotional vitality that come with age. The Russian lyric poet and novelist Boris Pasternak wrote his first novel, *Dr. Zhivago*, at the age of sixty-six. Susan B. Anthony, the famous social reformer and women's suffrage leader and pioneer, remained internationally active into her eighties, founding the International Woman

Suffrage Alliance in Berlin at age eighty-four. Born in 1939, Canadian writer-author Margaret Atwood's book *The Handmaiden's Tale*, published in 1985, re-emerged to great acclaim in 2018 and was followed by a sequel called *The Testaments* in 2019 bringing the author's work to the attention of a worldwide audience.

Margaret Atwood
By Larry D. Moore/CC BY-SA
creativecommons.org/
licenses/by-sa/4.0

AARP magazine, which is geared towards the issues of concern to older citizens, always features an older celebrity or public figure on its cover every month. While these highly visible individuals may be uniquely talented in the realm of their public endeavors, they aren't at all unique in the vitality they bring to life during their advancing years. All we have to do is take the time to look around to see people in all walks of life that are outstanding examples of aging with grace and vitality. One of my favorite writing clients was 92 years old when she published her memoir.

There is no denying that health complications are a part of life for many older people and that the risk of chronic disease or disabilities often does increase with age. And, Seniors were more at risk of death from the COVID-19 pandemic that struck in March of 2020. Obviously, there are wide ranging physical, mental and emotional aspects of aging. Nevertheless, we find all around us ample evidence that the creative spirit finds expression despite obstacles, grief, and loss at any age. The secret of living life with one's entire being can be traced to the creative spirit that dwells in each of us; it is found in our essence or our soul. When we live a soul-filled life, we go beyond the nomenclatures of gender, age, race, religion, income or health status, and can participate in life as a journey of continual exploration, discovery, and self-expression as well as self-acceptance of the changes that the aging process brings. Is it easy? Not necessarily. Some might say, "not at all." *Growing Old Ain't for Sissies!* was not only a best-selling book some years ago but also became a popular slogan seen printed on cards and tee-shirts worn by older folks.

Many years ago I worked as a facilitator for a program called Elderhostel, now known as Road Scholar Elderhostel, which is an educational and travel program for seniors. Road Scholar offers seniors opportunities to travel inexpensively to places throughout the United States as well as internationally where they usually stay in university dorms or other low-cost accommodations. Experts from all fields teach the seniors about the history and culture of the particular area they're visiting through classes, lectures, and field trips. On Maui where I worked as a facilitator, the Road Scholar Elderhostel program educated the participants in Hawaiian culture, ocean and marine mammal environments, and field trips to historical Hawaiian sites. Participants had to submit their medical records in advance so that the facilitator could be aware of their medical needs and conditions. When I first reviewed the medical records, I was stunned at the disabilities and physical impairments that most of the Elderhostel participants had written on their forms. Heart bypasses, lung diseases, cancer, and medications of seemingly infinite varieties. During the first evening, which was a group orientation. I expected to see a group of broken down seniors, hardly able to walk or talk. Instead, I saw a group of folks who were bright-eyed, inquisitive, alert, smart and funny! Throughout the entire two weeks of the Elderhostel excursion, no one ever complained or even mentioned any of their disabilities or illnesses. They were living in the moment and enjoying themselves. Working with elders helped me to re-evaluate how I felt about aging and to shift my ideas of what I thought I knew to be true about them.

I was so inspired, in fact, that I created and taught at the Maui Community College/continuing education a class called *Creating New Maps for Mid-Life*, which attracted a wide variety of people of all ages. Most of the people attending were interested in the challenge of mid-life that I had identified as being the time to discover a new dream for life's second half or final cycle. Many participants felt that they hadn't lived their dreams during the first half of their lives and didn't want to miss out on discovering and living their dreams for the second or final part. We spent time each class exploring how they got to where they were and where and what they wanted to be doing in the future, much as we have done in the earlier phases of the *Writes of Passage* journey. Those participants in their 70s and 80s were especially interested in discovering what a new dream for their final cycle could be, which turned out to be very inspirational to the other students.

WRITING EXERCISE: Getting Started Again

Revisit your retirement dreams and ask yourself if what you envisioned at the start truly fits what you have learned about yourself in the course of our autobiographical explorations through Writes of Passage. If you are an elder now or will be soon, are you willing to "test the waters" again and experiment, take some chances, make mistakes and pursue a notion simply because something about it tickles your fancy? As you answer these questions, be aware of the resistance factors once you dream of new paths, such as "I'm too old to do this," or, "I'm going to get started on this, just not right now, maybe next year."

> Write about the resistance factors you may be feeling about taking new paths or doing new things.

Wisdom Keepers

One of the most important roles for an elder is that of Wisdom Keeper. Elders long to pass on their wisdom gleaned from many years of living and life experiences. We are much richer as people and a culture when we honor our elders and invite them to share their wisdom with us.

Elders have always been seen as the holders of wisdom to primal people throughout the world. Two cultures that still hold elders in high esteem are Native American Indians and the Hawaiian culture in the Pacific Islands. The entire community belonging to these cultures look to elders for guidance and wisdom. In Hawaii, the *Kumulipo* is a genealogical creation chant that was composed around the eighteenth century. A modern elder named Rubellite Kawena Johnson has made the study of this myth her life's work, which resulted in her being  named a Wisdom Keeper to the Hawaiian people. She worked on the chant's translation for more than thirty years, bringing her expertise in science as well as theology to her pursuit of truth and knowledge from a global perspective. Not only has Professor Johnson been honored as an esteemed elder and Wisdom Keeper, but she continued the Hawaiian tradition of honoring the ancestors by beginning her translation of the *Kumulipo*, with a quote by an *Alii*, or ancient Hawaiian Royalty, named Liholiho: "Who would not be wise on the road long traveled by my ancestors?"

Many Native American cultures observe a wisdom path for living one's life called the Medicine Way. This pathway is reflected in the form of a circle called the Medicine Wheel, often constructed of stones laid out in a circle on the ground. Medicine Wheels can be found around the world from the great stone circles of Europe to the temple mandalas of India. Medicine Wheels are intended as places to pray, contemplate and strengthen one's place in nature by stimulating a better understanding of relations with all of creation.

Each stone within the Native American Medicine Wheel represents one of the many aspects of the Universe. There are stones representing the self, other members of the family, animals, and the four directions. At the center of the Medicine Wheel is a Creator stone, seen as the center of all life, which has no beginning or ending, and is always moving like a wheel.

Elders work with members of their community by helping them to understand that each person will journey around the Medicine Wheel many times in their lifetime, passing through the energies that each direction on the wheel represents. For example, the direction of the East represents the rising sun, place of illumination, new beginnings and the child; the South represents trust and innocence, place of adolescence and youth; the West, represents death and rebirth, and the adult; and the North represents strength and wisdom and is the place of elders. As each individual travels around the Medicine Wheel, they will experience life from as many of the positions as possible. If a person circumnavigates or dances the wheel with awareness, then they are able to heal themselves as they make the journey.

WRITING EXERCISE: Wisdom Keeper

As elders and keepers of wisdom, it is important to take on the role of mentor to help and influence others. Write about two things, ideas or values you shared with your family, friends, or colleagues that you are especially proud of in your life. Are there other ways that you can think of that you would like to share your knowledge and wisdom?

> Giving and receiving love is important on all levels of our being. Write a letter to someone telling them what they have meant to you and how much you love them.

Scared of Getting Older

Popular singer and songwriter John Mayer recorded a CD called *Continuum*, which has a song entitled "Stop This Train." The lyrics of this song talk about his fear of getting older. "So scared of getting older, I'm only good at being young, So I play the numbers game, To find a way to say that life has just begun." Mayer's lyrics express well not only what many younger people feel about death but older persons as well. At some point, however, we all must face our fear of dying. Once you are an elder, facing your own death becomes a necessity if you want to "die well," which according to many religious traditions means dying peacefully.

WRITING EXERCISE: "Today Is A Good Day To Die"

> We in the West don't like to think about death very much and we do everything we can to avoid discussing it. The Navajo Indians, however, have a saying, "Today is a good day to die." Write your response to this thought in your workbook.

> Think about what you would like for your grave marker to read; then write out what it would say. Here is what a grave marker of a gunslinger buried in Boothill cemetery in Tombstone, Arizona, reads: "Be what you is cuz if you be what you ain't, then you ain't what you is."

____

____

____

____

____

____

____

> If you're planning on being cremated, write about how you would like your remains to be handled and if you'd like any kind of ceremony to be performed. Take a moment to think about any preparations you've made for your dying and death.

____

____

____

____

____

____

____

____

> Make Your Wishes Known: Have you made a "living will" to help those you leave behind when you die to know what you'd like to have happen? Many people have chosen a document called "Five Wishes," which is also about advance care planning but is helpful in many other ways, too. It is not only a legal document but it is a complete approach to discussing and documenting your care and comfort choices. It's about connecting families, communication with healthcare providers and showing your community what it means to care for one another. Visit their website at https://fivewishes.org and download their free legally binding document.

> Write about how you would like to be remembered. *The Tibetan Book of the Dead* describes many Buddhist rituals, prayers and preparation necessary to die a good death, meaning to die without fear. Write about any fears you have about death and dying.

Why is it Good to Be Old?

It's important to remember as we become an elder that life is a process, something we'll want to keep thinking about, refining, and experimenting with until we die. Periodically reviewing your journal entries and other exercises from your *Writes of Passage* journey can refresh your memory as to what's important to you and can be a source for recharging your creativity in continuing to find those new pathways to invigorating your soul!

May Sarton was giving a lecture once right after her seventieth birthday. Someone in the audience asked her, "Why is it good to be old?" "Because," she answered, "I am more myself than I have ever been."

BIBLIOGRAPHY & SELECTED READING

"I never travel without my diary.
One should always have something sensational to read in the train."
~Oscar Wilde

Adams, Kathleen. *Journal to the Self: Twenty-Two Paths to Personal Growth.* New York: Warner Books, Inc., 1990.

Andrews, Lynn. *Teachings Around the Sacred Wheel: Finding the Soul of the Dreamtime.* Harper-San Francisco, 1990.

Baldwin, Christina. *Storycatcher: Making Sense of Our Lives Through the Power and Practice of Story.* Novato, Ca., New World Library, 2005.
One to One: Self-Understanding Through Journal Writing. New York: M Evans & Co., 1991.

Boldt, Laurence G. *Zen and the Art of Making a Living: A Practical Guide to Creative Career Design.* New York: Penguin/Arkana, 1999.

Briggs, John and David Peat. *Seven Life Lessons of Chaos: Spiritual Wisdom from the Science of Change.* New York: Harper-Collins, 1999.

Campbell, Joseph. Edited by Phil Cousineau. *The Hero's Journey.* New York: Harper & Row, 1990.

Cameron, Julia. *The Artist's Way.* New York: Jeremy P. Tarcher, 1992

Castaneda, Carlos. *The Fire Within.* New York: Pocket Books, 1984.

Diehn, Gwen. *The Decorated Journal.* New York: Lark Books, 2005.

Eisler, Riane. *The Chalice and the Blade.* San Francisco: Harper, 1987.

Ellis, Normandi. *Dreams of Isis: A Woman's Spiritual Sojourn.* Wheaton, Illinois: Quest Books, 1995.

Evans-Wentz, W. Y. *The Tibetan Book of the Dead.* New York: Oxford University Press, 1960.

Feinstein, David, and Stanley Krippner. *Personal Mythology: Using Ritual, Dreams, and Imagination to Discover Your Inner Story.* Los Angeles: Jeremy Tarcher, 1988.

Foster, Steven and Meredith Little. *The Book of Vision Quest: Personal Transformation in the Wilderness.* California: Island Press, 1980.

Hillman, James. *The Soul's Code: In Search of Character and Calling.* New York: Random House, 1996.

King, Stephen. *A Memoir of the Craft On Writing.* New York: Scribner, 2000.

Luhan, Mabel Dodge. *Edge of Taos Desert: An Escape to Reality.* University of New Mexico Press, 1965

May, Rollo. *The Cry for Myth.* New York: Bantam Doubleday, 1991.

Myers, Linda Joy. *The Power of Memoir: How to Write Your Healing Story.* San Francisco: Jossey-Bass, 2010.

Pennebaker, James. *Opening Up: The Healing Power of Expressing Emotions.* New York: The Guilford Press, 1990.

Pinkola-Estes, Clarissa. *Women Who Run With the Wolves.* New York: Ballantine Books, 1992.

Plotkin, Bill. *Nature and the Human Soul.* Novato, CA.: New World Library, 2008.

Raab, Diana M. *Writers and Their Notebooks.* University of South Carolina Press, 2010.

Rainer, Tristine. *The New Diary: How to Use a Journal for Self-Guidance & Expanded Creativity.* Los Angeles: Jeremy Tarcher, 2004.

St. Clair, Marjorie. *Wild Women Write: Re-Connecting with the Wild Feminine.* Albuquerque: Earth Muse Press, 2019.

Starhawk. *Dreaming the Dark: Magic, Sex & Politics.* Boston: Beacon Press, 1999.

See, Carolyn. *Making a Literary Life: Advice for Writers and Other Dreamers.* New York: Ballantine Books, 2002.

Sun Bear. *Dancing with the Wheel.* New York: Simon & Schuster, 1991.

Toms, Michael and Justine. *True Work.* New York: Bell Tower, 1999.

Ueland, Brenda. *If You Want to Write: A Book about Art, Independence & Spirit.* BN Publishing, 2010.

Vogler, Christopher. *The Writers Journey: Mythic Structure for Writers.* Studio City, CA.: Michael Wiese Productions, 1998.

ABOUT THE AUTHOR

Marjorie St. Clair is a writing teacher and coach who helps writers discover their passion and purpose through the power of writing from the heart. This is her second writing workbook. Her first workbook *Wild Women Write: Re-Connecting With the Wild Feminine* was highly praised by writers and those interested in the Wild Woman archetype.

For years she has facilitated annual writing retreats at the historical Mabel Dodge Luhan House in Taos, NM as well as Ghost Ranch.* For more information on writing retreats, classes and coaching or to contact her, visit www.writersadventure.com. Follow her on Facebook and Instagram.

Author at Mabel Dodge Luhan Inn, Taos, NM

---

* Coming in 2021, a Writing Retreat on the beautiful island of Maui!